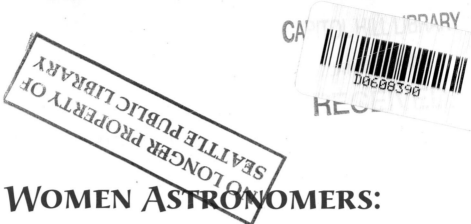

# WOMEN ASTRONOMERS:

# REACHING FOR THE STARS

Women Astronomers: Reaching for the Stars
Copyright 2008 by Stone Pine Press, Inc.
Marcola, Oregon

The purpose of the book is educational and there is no intent to violate rights. Diligent effort has been made to contact copyright holders. Where found, they are cited in the Credits section. Questions should be addressed to the publisher.

Printed in the United States of America

Library of Congress Cataloging-in-Publication Data

Armstrong, Mabel.
  Women astronomers : reaching for the stars / Mabel Armstrong.
    p. cm.
  Includes bibliographical references and index.
  ISBN 978-0-9728929-5-7 (trade paper : alk. paper)  1. Women astronomers.
2. Women in astronomy--History. I. Title.

QB34.5.A76 2007
508.2--dc22
                        2007022318


ISBN  978-0-97289295-7

Book and Cover Design by Niki Harris Graphic Design

The front cover background photograph, *The Heart of the Milky Way*, was taken July 25, 2003, by Sam Pitts, near Veneta, Oregon. The bright center just above the front of the telescope is the center core area of our Milky Way Galaxy. The scope is pointed at the constellation of Sagittarius and the bright yellow-red star above the girl's head is Antares, the heart of the constellation of Scorpius.

For hands-on astronomy activities go to www.womenastronomers.com

# WOMEN ASTRONOMERS:
# REACHING FOR THE STARS

Women
have
always
studied
the
night
sky.

## MABEL ARMSTRONG

Discovering Women in Science Series

# DEDICATION

For the next generations of women astronomers with thanks and gratitude to those who went before.

# Acknowledgments

This project has accumulated many debts to those who helped, supported and encouraged me along the way.

Amanda Marusich and Brittany Sundberg critiqued early drafts from the perspective of the target readers. Brenda Shaw Weakley searched the Dundee, Scotland, town records for information on Williamina Fleming. Hayden Hodges and Alice Kaseberg helped me get the math and physics right, and directed my attention to issues I might have missed. Dr. John Percy at the University of Toronto tracked down images and astronomers. Christine Sundt was especially generous with her time and expertise in consulting about visual resources.

Dr. Vera Rubin and Dr. Nancy Roman graciously shared personal photographs.

Archivists and special collections librarians at Wellesley, Mount Holyoke, Vassar and Harvard searched their collections for appropriate images and made them available.

A special thank you to all those who make stunning astronomical images available online. The images from the Hubble Space Telescope, and other observatories awe and inspire. Without you this would have been a very different book.

Editors Polly Bowman, Elizabeth Lyon, and Vickie Nelson pushed, pulled, tweaked, and honed my fuzzy thoughts into a publishable manuscript. Various writers' workshops and critique groups pushed and prodded the work toward its final form. You know who you are, and I'm grateful for your interest and your efforts.

Designer Niki Harris created the look of the book, gathered everything together with great attention to detail and personal devotion, and navigated the complex electronic path to the printer.

Thank you all for your time, interest and energy. If, despite your efforts, errors have crept into the book, they are of my own making.

# CONTENTS

# List of Sidebars

# Introduction

Women have always studied the night sky. Five thousand years ago, priestesses studied the stars and planets as a way to forecast human and heavenly events. Yet the names of most of these women have been lost. One exception is EnHeduanna, a high ranking astronomer-priestess in Babylon, although it is her poetry which survives to the present. Better known by far is Hypatia of Alexandria. And even in her case, the amount of information we have is tiny compared to her status in the ancient world. It is as if we could see two thousand years into the future and find that no one remembers anything about Albert Einstein except his name.

From Hypatia's death around 370 CE to Caroline Herschel's career in the late 1700s and early 1800s, information about women in science nearly disappeared from Western history. Belief in astrology largely replaced the study of astronomy. Most of those who observed the night sky looked for omens and portents. A few people tried to understand the motion of planets and stars. But they lacked the equipment that would let them see, and the mathematics that would let them understand what they saw.

In some Eastern countries, women continued to study astronomy. Queen Sondok, of Korea, built an observatory around 680 CE. We know little about her life, although the observatory still stands.

## Dates

BCE stands for "before the common era," and CE, for the "common era." The new names are culturally neutral and correspond to BC and AD from the Gregorian calendar.

Women have always studied the night sky.

Nearly a thousand years passed before Caroline Herschel, the first woman astronomer in the modern sense of the word, helped change the science forever. Once Caroline and her brother William began to do sound astronomical research, in the late 1770s, astronomy blossomed as a science.

In order to develop theories about the behavior of heavenly bodies, scientists needed enormous amounts of data. From 1890 through the early 1940s, women, especially those who worked for the Harvard Observatory, supplied most of those data. The observatory jobs, though low paid, were more attractive than working in cotton mills or as maids.

By the early 1920s, major U.S. universities began to award doctorates in astronomy, a sure sign that astronomy had gained acceptance as a true science. Cecilia Payne Gaposchkin, who discovered that stars are made almost entirely of hydrogen, earned the first astronomy PhD awarded by Harvard Observatory. She was quickly followed by Helen Sawyer Hogg, one of Canada's most famous astronomers.

Resistance to educating women in the sciences increased rapidly, however. By the 1930s most major universities refused even to admit women to undergraduate physics programs, the first requirement for a graduate degree in astronomy. In the 1980s Federal legislation opened university programs to women, and their numbers began to increase in all sciences. By the turn of the twenty-first century, many more women were doing astronomy than are included in this book.

All the women profiled here struggled with society's narrow ideas of women's appropriate roles — bearing children, running households, and keeping a low profile. Each woman's challenges were different, and each met the challenges in her own way. Every woman would surely tell you, however, that she would do it all over again. The enormous joy each experienced, or continues to experience, in her chosen field is reflected in Vera Rubin's story. Her son asked if she actually got paid for the fun she had at work. ◉

# Women Astronomers of Ancient Times

In ancient times, astronomical events such as eclipses and comets frightened many people. Those who could predict such events were thought to have mystical powers. They were often priests and priestesses and enjoyed high positions in society. EnHeduanna was an early astronomer-priestess.

Around 2350 BCE, King Sargon of Babylonia appointed his daughter to a high position. He gave her the title Chief Astronomer Priestess of the Moon Goddess of the City. We don't know her birth name, but the priestesses she supervised called her EnHeduanna, meaning "ornament of heaven." Her position and name tell us that she was a skilled astronomer.

## ENHEDUANNA
### lived around 2350 BCE

As Chief Astronomer Priestess, EnHeduanna supervised one of the world's first big bureaucracies. She managed a large network of temples and observatories staffed by other astronomer-priestesses. These priestesses used the movement of the stars to create calendars. In early Babylon, calendars directed all the activities of society. Calendars showed the best times for religious festivals and planting crops. When Babylonians wanted to travel or get married, they used the calendar to find a time that would bring them good luck. The calendar the priestesses of Babylon created is still used today to set the dates of religious events, such as Easter. ◉

*Greek mythology*

*Maya 500 BCE*

*France 1683*

## Ancient Calendars

Early humans knew that the Sun, Moon, and stars moved in regular patterns. Knowing that a full Moon happened periodically, and that the Sun rose over a particular rock every so many days, led people to devise ways to quantify the passage of time. Archeologists studying Ice Age sites in Europe have found 20,000-year-old bones containing holes drilled in patterns that suggest they were used to count the days between phases of the Moon. The stones at Stonehenge in England are aligned with the path of the Sun on the summer solstice. And in the New World, Mayan and Aztec stone calendars used the Sun, the Moon, and the planet Venus as a basis for defining the length and divisions of a year.

*Egypt 54 BCE*

*Aztec 1200*

*Stonehenge in England 2500 BCE*

*China 1000 CE*

Early civilizations viewed physics, math, astronomy, and their applications as a single field they called natural philosophy. Hypatia's skill in all these arenas was not surprising. The fact that she was a woman skilled in all, and was also an outstanding teacher, a civic leader, and a political rebel besides, is still surprising.

*To teach superstition as truth is a most terrible thing.*

*Hypatia*

# HYPATIA

**born 370**

**died 415**

One of the women astronomers we know a bit about was a Greek woman, Hypatia, who lived in Alexandria, Egypt, around the fourth century CE. She is known to us almost entirely through letters from her students. Some of these students almost worshiped her, and their praises may be overblown. Other accounts of Hypatia's life come from people on one side or the other of the civil and political upheavals that disturbed Alexandria during her lifetime. Many of the people who reviled her, however, did so because of the philosophical or political positions she took.

When Hypatia was born, her father, Theon, was a professor of mathematics and astronomy in Alexandria. He believed, as many Greeks did, that it was possible to raise a perfect human being. He seems to have thought Hypatia would be a good subject.

To mold Hypatia into perfection, Theon gave her the best possible education, including studies in mathematics, languages, rhetoric, and natural philosophy, or science. She also learned to swim, ride horses, climb mountains, and row a boat. Perfection, to the Greeks, included an active, healthy body.

Some writers say that when Theon decided there was nothing left for Hypatia to learn in Alexandria, he sent her to study in Greece and Italy. She traveled for another ten years throughout the rest of Europe, meeting

## The Library at Alexandria

Early in the third century BCE, Ptolemy II of Egypt built a huge library and academy in Alexandria containing a half million books and lecture seating for five thousand students. Together, the academy and library became the world center for study and scholarship.

Ptolemy III added to the library holdings by confiscating all scrolls that travelers brought to the city. He had the writings copied. Then he shelved the originals in the library and gave the copies to the original owners.

By the end of the fourth century CE, the library and all academic buildings had been destroyed. Historians disagree on the causes, but invasions, civil war, and religious strife all seem to have contributed. The great loss of knowledge caused one historian to remark that if the library at Alexandria had not been destroyed, the industrial revolution would have occurred 1500 years earlier.

and studying with the most famous mathematicians and philosophers of the time.

According to history, Hypatia impressed everyone she met with her intellect and her beauty.

When Hypatia returned to Alexandria, she found a job at the most famous institution in the ancient world, the library at Alexandria. She became a teacher at a time when few women had any public role. She taught mathematics, physics, and astronomy, and wrote many books about these subjects. For example, she wrote thirteen books on algebra, her favorite subject, and another eight books on geometry. The books she wrote were in the form of scrolls. The information in each scroll would fill only fifty or sixty pages of one of today's textbooks.

Unfortunately, most of Hypatia's books were lost when the museum burned during years of civil war.

Hypatia liked to apply her knowledge of physics by inventing tools and astronomical devices. Two of her inventions undoubtedly saved the lives of many sailors. She invented an apparatus for distilling drinkable water from sea water, a boon for sailors who were often far from land and fresh water. She also designed an astrolabe, an instrument used to measure the positions of the stars, another important tool for sailors.

4000 BCE

Egyptians use a 360-day calendar divided into twelve months of thirty days each.

*The Great Library of Alexandria* by O. Von Corven.

3000 BCE

The Women's School at Sao, Egypt, teaches medicine to men and women.

The astrolabe let them locate specific stars and use the stars' positions for navigation.

*An astrolabe*

She used her astrolabe to calculate the positions of specific stars, and then published her data in tables. Sailors and astronomers used her tables of positions of the stars, *Astronomical Canon,* for the next 1200 years.

Hypatia was a popular teacher and public lecturer, and soon became known across the civilized world as a sage and a scholar. Her books and public lectures were so well known that she often received letters addressed just to: "Philosopher, Alexandria."

One of Hypatia's students wrote about her: "The magistrates consulted her first in their administration of the affairs of the City." She was a close friend of Orestes, the Roman governor of Egypt. This friendship landed her in the middle of serious political tensions and led to her early death.

Alexandria was under the rule of strong leaders in Rome who were adopting Christianity and insisting that all citizens convert. Hypatia refused to adopt Christianity. She clung to the teachings of Plato and lectured publicly about Neoplatonism, a philosophy that encourages people to question everything.

In her classes and public lectures, Hypatia exhorted people to think critically. "Reserve your right to think," she said. "For even to think wrongly is better than not to think at all." She also said, "To teach superstitions as truth is a most terrible thing."

Hypatia's pronouncements were unpopular with the more conservative segment of society, not only because they flew in the face of religious edicts from Rome, but because she said them publicly. Upper-class women of the time were usually secluded, expected to devote themselves solely to husband and children.

2772 BCE

Women supervise state-owned perfume and textile industries in Egypt.

Hypatia's public position and growing influence with city leaders angered many. Powerful men in the church were especially upset about her friendship with Orestes. When Hypatia sided with Orestes in a power struggle with Cyril, the head of the Christian Church in Alexandria, her enemies decided to silence her. An angry mob, some say sent by Cyril, attacked and murdered her. They beat her with stones, cut her with clam shells, and finally burned her body.

The death of Hypatia, and the loss of the world's largest collection of scientific and mathematic writings, brought scientific advances in the West almost to a halt for nearly a thousand years. This time of little scientific or social advancement lasted from about 400 to 1400 CE, and became known as the Dark Ages. ◉

## The Korean Astronomer Queen

Ancient trade routes spread information as well as merchandise. Some women in Asia became as skilled as those in Babylon and Greece.

Queen Sondok ruled the kingdom of Silla in Korea beginning in 632 CE. As a skilled astronomer, Queen Sondok predicted eclipses of the Sun and Moon. She calculated the date of the equinoxes: the two times of the year, in Spring and Fall, when the sun crosses the plane of the earth's equator and day and night are of equal length. Because of her skill, the calendars used in Silla were the most accurate of their time.

Sondok built the Chonsongdae Observatory, the oldest remaining astronomical observatory in the Far East. The observatory was built with 365 stones, one for each day of the year. Because she was the 27th ruler of her province of Silla, she made it 27 stones high. And it stands on a platform made of 12 tiles for the 12 months of the calendar.

Aganice studies the constellations in Egypt.

## Timekeeping by the Sun

Around five thousand years ago, developing cultures began to need ways to measure the passage of time in periods smaller than days and months. People also needed ways to set meeting times for religious and business purposes. They needed clocks.

Some of the earliest clocks still in existence are obelisks, the Sun clocks of the Egyptians, in use by 1500 BCE. The shadow cast by the tall stone pillar separated the day into morning and afternoon based on which side of the pillar the shadow was on. The length of the shadow corresponded roughly to the hour.

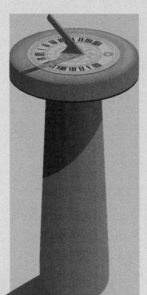

Improvements on the obelisk produced many designs, and by 30 BCE, at least thirteen different sundial styles were in use in Greece and Asia Minor. Because most of these timepieces were large objects, they were installed on the surface of buildings, or in courtyards or parks. Demand for portable timepieces produced personal sundials. Henry VIII, the king of England, wore a sundial ring. Bracelets and lockets were also popular sundial designs among the wealthy.

You can build your own sundial using one of the designs on this web site: www.sundials.co.uk/projects.htm

2,350 BCE

2,000 BCE

EnHeduanna appointed Chief Astronomer Priestess of the Moon Goddess of Babylon.

Queen Zipporah sends a botanical expedition to look for new medicinal plants.

European convents and monasteries became centers for education and study during the Middle Ages. Most scientists and physicians, both women and men, belonged to religious orders. One of the best known was Hildegard.

## The Sybil of the Rhine

Some small sparks of light did shine through the Dark Ages in Europe. In 1098, a little girl was born who would make her name in music and theology as well as science. Hildegard was born into a wealthy family living in Bickelheim, on the banks of the Nahe River in Germany. She was a sickly child who suffered from stomach ailments, fevers, and headaches. Her father finally sent Hildegard to a small Benedictine convent where her Aunt Jutta was abbess. Convents often had the best medical services of the time, and Hildegard's family must have hoped the regular hours, healthy food, and her aunt's attention would help Hildegard get well.

# HILDEGARD OF BINGEN

**born 1098**

**died 1179**

Life in the convent didn't improve Hildegard's health as much as everyone hoped, and she suffered from poor health all her life. Scholars now think she may have had epilepsy or migraines.

The convent did give Hildegard an education. She was an eager student who took advantage of every opportunity to learn. She studied medicine, botany, music, philosophy, and theology, and she spoke several languages. She had a consuming interest in cosmology, which is the study of the universe, or cosmos. When Jutta died, Hildegard took charge of the convent.

Before long, Hildegard decided that administering the convent took far too much time from her other interests. There were visiting pilgrims to house, local politics to deal with, and a large and growing convent to administer. Soon

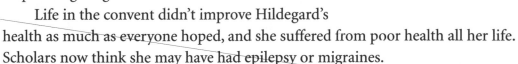

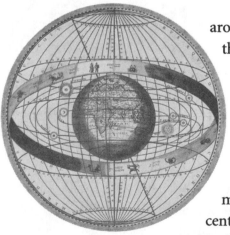

she had a vision telling her to go to a small neighboring town. Here she founded and built the Bingen Convent.

In 1150, Hildegard opened her new convent with eighteen young women. Unfortunately, the move didn't bring Hildegard the peace she sought. The move and the new convent's rapid growth caused her great stress, and she was ill for many years afterward.

Despite her health problems, Hildegard studied constantly and wrote prolifically. She wrote letters to all the leading thinkers of the time, including emperors, popes, bishops, nuns, and nobles. She published several works describing her theories of the universe. Many of her ideas came straight from the Pythagoreans, who imagined that the earth was surrounded by crystal shells that held the stars in place. Hildegard named the shells water, air, and fire.

**Hildegard believed that the Earth revolved around the Sun, at a time when most people believed the Earth was the center of the universe.**

Hildegard believed that the Earth revolved around the Sun, at a time when most people believed that the Earth was the center of the universe and that the Sun, along with all other heavenly bodies, circled the Earth. Hildegard's theory of the solar system was ignored for three hundred years, until Copernicus published his work suggesting the same thing.

Hildegard's fame was primarily due to her medical writings and her musical compositions. For centuries she was Germany's most important medical writer. Despite her poor health, she lived to be eighty-one years old and died in 1179. ◉

Babylonian and Chinese astronomers describe planetary movement.

# Astronomy Becomes Science

In 1610, Galileo pointed the first telescope at the night sky and started a revolution in astronomy. Caroline Herschel furthered that revolution through a lifetime spent helping her brother William build bigger and better telescopes. And, by establishing a regular, systematic schedule of observing the night sky and carefully recording all data, Caroline changed the very nature of observational astronomy.

*Her fame will be held*
*in honour through all ages.*

French astronomer Pierre-Francois-Andre Mechain

## CAROLINE LUCRETIA HERSCHEL

**born 1750**

**died 1848**

Fourteen-year-old Caroline Herschel stood on tiptoe and peeked out the window into the courtyard below. She wished she could be down there with her father and her brother William. Her mother had given her a long list of chores to do this morning. She hoped she could finish in time.

Caroline watched as Papa and Willie helped some of the younger Herschel boys fill a large tub with water. Today Hanover, Germany, the city where the Herschels lived, would see a total eclipse of the Sun. For several minutes the Moon would be directly between the Earth and Sun. The Sun would vanish completely, except for a glowing halo. People who stared directly

**How to Watch a Solar Eclipse**

Caroline Herschel's father knew that looking directly at the Sun could damage his children's eyes. In order for his children to see the eclipse without looking at the Sun, Isaac Herschel used a tub of water as a mirror. The family could watch the eclipse in reflection.

Using a pinhole camera is another way to watch an eclipse while protecting our eyes. And it is easier to handle than a tub of water. To make a pinhole camera, we'll need a thin piece of cardboard, such as the one on the back of a writing tablet, and a sheet of white paper. First, we make a small hole in the center of the piece of cardboard with a large needle or a safety pin. We then hold the cardboard between the Sun and the sheet of white paper. The sun shines through the hole and onto the paper. Look for the image of the Sun on the paper. Then move the cardboard around until the image is clear.

We may see dark spots in the image of the Sun projected onto the piece of paper. Those are sunspots, places where solar flares are occurring. Pinhole cameras are useful for following sunspots as they move across the surface of the Sun as well as for watching eclipses.

at the eclipse would hurt their eyes. Papa and William had a clever plan, however. Using the big tub as a reflecting pool, the family could safely watch the eclipse reflected in the water.

Earlier this morning, as she helped Mama serve breakfast, Caroline had taken a deep breath. Then, she had asked for permission to watch the eclipse with the family. Mama hadn't said no yet, but she hadn't said yes, either. Her mother, like many people at that time, didn't think girls needed to know about comets and eclipses. Girls just needed to know how to cook and clean. But today, Mama was in a good mood. Her oldest son, William, was back home in Germany after seven long years away in England.

When Caroline heard Mama calling her, she sighed, left the window, and hurried up the stairs to finish cleaning. She did not want to make her mother angry today.

Caroline had had a difficult childhood. She was the eighth of ten children born to the unhappy marriage of Anna and Isaac Herschel. Anna and Isaac disagreed about many things. Most importantly for Caroline, they disagreed about education. Isaac was a talented musician and an enthusiastic amateur astronomer who valued education highly. Anna could not read or write.

Worse, she believed educating children simply caused trouble. She grudgingly allowed Isaac to educate their sons, but would not let him teach Caroline more than reading and writing.

Caroline had other strikes against her. At age four, she had survived a bout with smallpox that left her face badly scarred. Then she contracted typhus. The disease limited her growth so that at fourteen, she stood just a bit over four feet tall. As a tiny, unattractive teenager, Caroline thought she probably wouldn't ever marry. Her mother wouldn't let her learn French or any other skill that would help her find work as a governess. Without a husband or some way to support herself, Caroline expected to spend her life working as an unpaid servant for her family.

Even her affectionate father feared for her future. He told her it was unlikely any man would make her an offer of marriage. Perhaps, he added to soften the blow, later in her life some old man might take her for her good qualities. His words dismayed Caroline and made her long for financial independence. Then she wouldn't need an old man for a husband. She could support herself.

Actually, despite Mama's efforts, Caroline was already a budding musician. Papa gave violin and horn lessons to a steady stream of students. And he often defied his wife and secretly included Caroline in the lessons. What Isaac didn't teach her about music, Caroline absorbed just by living in a house where students were constantly practicing.

Besides her loving father, the other bright spot in Caroline's young life was her oldest brother, William. He shared Isaac Herschel's love of music and enthusiasm for mathematics and astronomy. Papa and William's excited conversations about science and math often lasted far into the night. Mama often yelled at them to quiet down because they were keeping the little ones awake.

***Maria Cunitz,*** who died fourteen years after Caroline Herschel was born, lived in Poland. She published the astronomical tables based on Kepler's tables. Her volume was published privately in 1650.

600 BCE

Chinese and Greeks use sundials.

300 BCE

Aristarchus postulates a Sun-centered universe.

William had left for England in 1761, when Caroline was only seven years old. How she had missed him! And now he was home in time for a total eclipse of the Sun. Caroline stopped sweeping as she heard Papa calling the family into the courtyard. Once again she peeked out the window. Mama was there standing next to William. With a smile, Caroline put away her dusting rags and ran to join her family.

Three years later, in 1767, Isaac Herschel died. Seventeen-year-old Caroline was devastated. With Papa gone and William in England, she had no emotional support left. And Mama was more difficult than ever. She seemed determined to stamp out any foolish notions Caroline might have developed from her father's lessons. She ordered Caroline to work as a servant for her brother Jacob, who fancied himself a man about town. Caroline cooked, cleaned, and waited on Jacob and his friends. Sometimes Jacob beat her, calling her slow and clumsy. William, however, had other plans for his sister.

As head musician for a large church in Bath, England, William knew many people in the musical community. He thought Caroline had a future as a professional singer. He wanted her to live with him and study music. For two years, William wrote to his mother trying to persuade her to let Caroline leave Germany. Finally, he agreed to send money home so his mother could hire a servant to replace Caroline. Anna then agreed to let her go. William came to Hanover in August, 1772, to take Caroline to England to live with him and another brother, Alexander.

At twenty-two, Caroline arrived in Bath. She spoke no English and was almost as bewildered and scared as she was excited and happy. She was also determined to earn her own way. She did not want to be a financial burden on William, who had

50 BCE                                                    370 CE

The Julian calendar is introduced with 365.25 days in each year.          Hypatia is born in Alexandria.

rescued her from a life of drudgery. She took over management of William's household. It was a big job, but one for which she had lots of practice. She supervised a cook, a maid, and a gardener. She shopped daily for food. At first, shopping was an ordeal. The shopkeepers' rapid English confused her. And she had trouble counting out change with the unfamiliar English coins. Months later, she discovered that her brother Alexander had followed her every day. He kept out of sight. He wanted to be nearby if shopkeepers tried to take advantage of her.

Besides running the household, Caroline helped William with his musical work. She scheduled lessons, rehearsed the choir, and copied arrangements. She practiced piano and voice on her own. It was a busy life, but Caroline was happy, living in England with a much-loved brother and contributing to his success.

Then the day came when Caroline was offered a contract to sing professionally. At last, her musical future seemed assured. Finally, she would be able to support herself. But now she had a difficult choice to make.

William's enthusiasm for astronomy was eating into his time. Every night he gobbled down his dinner. Then he rushed off to study physics or astronomy. When not closeted with books, he designed telescopes. Or he spent hours observing the night sky. Then he started building and selling telescopes as well.

Caroline loved her brother and knew she owed her freedom to him. She also knew he needed her help if he was to have time to study astronomy, carry out his observations, and build bigger and better telescopes. Many years later, she wrote, "My brother would have been very much at a loss but for my assistance." She gave up her chance at a musical career and devoted herself to helping William revolutionize astronomy.

Caroline may have been a tiny person, but she was a dynamo. She loved astronomy and threw herself into telescope

415 CE                    610 CE

Hypatia is murdered in Alexandria.          Queen Sondok of Korea builds observatory, Temple of the Moon and Stars

*Catherina Elisabetha Koopman was the second wife of amateur astronomer Johannes Hevelius. In this early engraving she is shown making observations with her husband.*

building. "I saw almost every room turned into a workshop," she wrote. "A cabinet maker making tubes and stands of all descriptions in a handsome furnished drawing-room. Alex putting up a huge turning machine in a bedroom for turning patterns, grinding glasses and turning eye-pieces."

The Herschels set out to transform the science of astronomy. First, they built telescopes that were bigger and better than any the world had known. Then, they used their telescopes to study the night sky in a completely new way. Caroline wrote, "William wanted to study the construction of the heavens. He was not content knowing what other observers had seen." Caroline became the recorder. As they scanned the sky systematically, she carefully entered all their data in her journals. In 1779, they began an ambitious project. They planned to identify and map every single object they saw in the night sky. In three years, they swept the sky three times. A sweep requires looking at every portion of the sky and recording the locations and times of appearance of all objects. In their first full sweep, they discovered the planet Uranus, the first new planet to be found in a thousand years.

William taught Caroline physics and math so she could do the calculations and proofread the papers he sent to other astronomers and to the Royal Academy. He called the math problems he designed for her "little lessons for Lina." By 1780, Caroline spoke two languages and knew astronomy and mathematics. Despite her mother's efforts to the contrary, she was better educated than most women in Europe.

A critical member of the Herschel team, Carolyn recorded observations and calculated star locations and movements. She compiled all the information into usable tables. She also reorganized the leading star catalog, listing stars by specific zones, based on degrees from the poles, rather than by constellation. In two catalogs, *The Index to the Catalogue of 860 Stars Observed by Flamsteed but Not Included in the British Catalogue,* and *Index to Every Observation of Every Star in the British Catalogue,* Caroline resolved many discrepancies found in earlier publications. She expanded the number of stars included in the catalogs. Then she designed an index that made the catalogs far more useful than they had been.

Using the enormous telescopes the Herschels built, astronomers suddenly found themselves looking at things they couldn't identify. Some objects appeared as fuzzy blobs. They called these blobs nebulae, from the word "nebulous," meaning undefined. These nebulae weren't stars or planets. And their discovery puzzled astronomers everywhere. Caroline's catalog of 2,600 nebulae ignited

***Mary Fairfax Somerville*** made a major contribution to astronomy. She translated French mathematician Henri Laplace's study of celestial mechanics into English. Somerville's 1813 publication, *The Mechanism of the Heavens,* carefully explained Laplace's new mathematics to English scientists. The book was a huge success. It established Mary Somerville as a leading astronomer-mathematician of her day. The book was the standard text in the field for a hundred years. Somerville College at Oxford is named for Mary Somerville.

## What Is a Nebula?

Charles Messier's 1780 catalog listed 103 nebulae, or fuzzy objects. By 1802, Caroline Herschel had added 2600 new nebulae and reorganized the *Messier Catalog*. For another 150 years, astronomers argued about what nebulae might be. The debate was not settled until the 1930s. But the discussions and theories put forth to explain nebulae helped advance our understanding of the universe.

Shown here is the planetary nebula NGC 6369, known to amateur astronomers as the "Little Ghost Nebula," because it looks like a small, ghostly cloud.

a world-wide debate about their identity. The debate advanced astronomy rapidly.

Astronomers were not the only people who wanted the new telescopes. Even George III, the King of England, had to have one. An enthusiastic amateur astronomer himself, King George gave William a small salary as a reward for discovering Uranus. Then the king asked the Herschels to move closer to the castle so they would be handy when he wanted astronomy lessons. The salary let the Herschels give up professional music. They left Bath and turned to full-time astronomy.

Caroline packed up the household and moved it to Windsor. When King George wanted them closer still, she moved again. This time they moved to the tiny town of

1609

Slough, north of Windsor. Here the Herschels turned their house into the foremost astronomical observatory of their time.

Every clear night, Caroline and William studied the heavens. He sat high above the house at a telescope. She sat below in a small, unheated room beside an open window so she could hear him. As William called out the position of each star, comet, or nebula, Caroline checked the star charts and recorded the information. A metronome ticked away at her side, keeping track of the time of passage of each object.

A visitor to the Herschel home wrote in his diary about an evening when the temperature dropped to twelve degrees Fahrenheit. The Herschels just put on more clothes. When Caroline's ink froze, she melted it over her candle and went on writing.

On nights they observed, she worked all night long and slept just a few hours in the early morning. During the day, she copied William's papers for publication and checked his computations. She wrote the directions for assembling the telescopes they sold, and designed and published the star catalogs.

Their telescopes grew larger along with Caroline's catalogs. They made huge polished-metal mirrors to gather and reflect light from distant stars. For their largest, a forty-eight-inch mirror, they melted many pounds of molten metal. They poured the liquid metal into a mold formed in a huge mound of soil and sand in the backyard. After casting, they polished the mirrors to a high gloss by hand. William polished the mirror for days at a

*The Ant Nebula was discovered in 1922. The strange shape of this nebula intrigues astronomers. The unusual length of the nebula—over a light-year long—and the 1000-kilometer-per-second speed with which gas is expelled from the central star, may be clues to the shape.*

Isaac Newton publishes *Principia Mathematica,* including the laws of planetary motion.

time, and Caroline spooned food into his mouth as he worked.

When they mounted the big mirror in a forty-foot-long tube, it became the largest telescope in the world. It was often called the eighth wonder of the world, and travelers came to Slough from all over the world to see it.

As William and Caroline's reputations grew, astronomers from around the world visited the Herschel home to exchange ideas and information. William also visited other astronomers, both in England and Europe. Caroline enjoyed meeting and talking with visiting scientists in her own home, but she hated

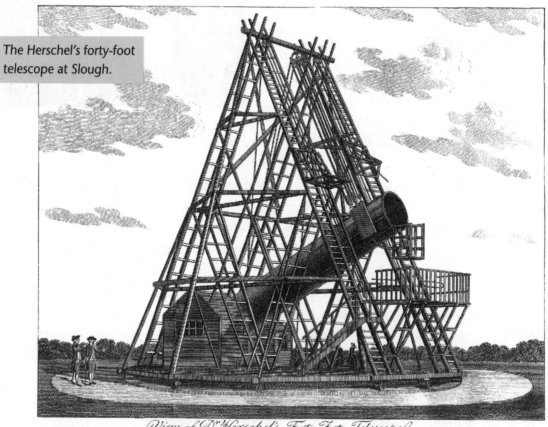

The Herschel's forty-foot telescope at Slough.

*View of Dr. Herschel's Forty Feet Telescope.*

1750

Caroline Herschel is born in Germany.

1771

Caroline goes to Bath, England, to live with her brother William.

# Fear of Comets

Our ancestors were afraid of comets because they appeared with no warning and no explanation. They seemed like dreadful omens, and people easily associated them with catastrophes such as plagues and earthquakes. People often blamed the death of a king or emperor on the appearance of a comet. Sometimes, the death and the comet were separated by months or even years. But that did not keep people from believing that comets were omens.

When English astronomer Edmund Halley studied the historic records of comet appearances, he noticed that the descriptions of one particular comet, seen in 1531, 1607, and 1682, seemed quite similar. He suggested that all three of these sightings were of the same comet. Then he went even further. He calculated the orbit of this comet and predicted its next visit to earth. When his prediction came true, the comet was named for him. Halley's Comet is due for a return visit in 2062.

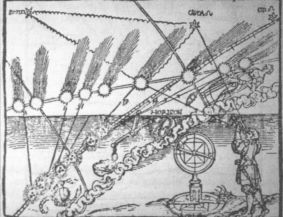

German astronomer Peter Apian observed that the tail of a comet always points away from the Sun.

As more comets returned as predicted, they began to lose their mystic importance. People thought of them as natural occurrences. Few people now believe comets foretell the death of powerful people or bring plagues. However, comets may cause catastrophe if they hit the Earth. In 1994, Carolyn Shoemaker watched as comet Shoemaker-Levy slammed into the planet Jupiter (see page 138).

Late in 1998, scientists found an impact crater that included pieces of glass that appeared to have come from a comet crashing into the Earth. Some scientists think this kind of impact killed off all the dinosaurs millions of years ago. Astronomers who worry about comets hitting the Earth have started programs to spot them as early as possible (see page 141).

1782

The Herschels leave Bath and turn to astronomy full time.

travel and seldom left Slough. She had little patience with tourists who came to see the sights without any interest in astronomy, even members of the royal court. In her diary, she referred to one lady-in-waiting as a "giggling ninny."

### Maria Margarethe Kirch and Christine Kirch

were the wife and daughter of Gottfried Kirch, who headed the Berlin Observatory in the early 18th century. While her husband was alive, Maria helped with his observations. After his death, Maria worked at other observatories. When their son became an observer at Berlin in 1716, she and Christine worked as his assistants, doing observations and calculations.

Caroline's life settled into a peaceful routine. But William had another surprise for her. In 1788, he married Mary Pitt, a widow who lived nearby. The marriage came as a shock to Caroline. Another woman now held first place in William's affections, and Caroline worried again about money. Where would she live? What would she eat? How could she clothe herself?

William solved Caroline's money concerns by persuading King George to give her a personal salary. Finally, in 1787, at the age of thirty-four, Caroline Herschel was financially independent. But she had become emotionally estranged from her brother.

Fortunately, William's new wife, Mary, was a warm, friendly woman who must have understood Caroline's feelings. Her kindness toward Caroline began to mend the rift caused by the marriage. And the birth of baby John helped. Caroline adored her nephew and delighted in helping him grow up to become an astronomer nearly as well known as his father.

### Caroline's Comet

When William traveled to Europe, Caroline scanned the night sky alone, sweeping for comets. In 1786, she spotted an object she knew had not been there the night before. "The object of last night *is a comet*," she wrote in her diary on August 2, 1786. With that note, she became the first woman in recorded history to discover a comet. She eventually discovered numerous nebulae and a total of nine comets, though not one was named for her.

1786

Caroline Herschel discovers her first comet. The Herschels move to Slough, England.

## You, Too, Could Discover a Comet

Looking for a comet is called comet sweeping. Astronomers know that comets often come out of certain areas of space. They check these sections of the sky every night. Astronomers are so familiar with the stars in these areas that they immediately recognize when a new object appears.

Comet sweepers look for rapidly moving, fuzzy objects. Comets are closer than stars and move very fast. Their positions seem to change rapidly, often in just a night or two.

The eighteenth century astronomer Charles Messier published a catalog of more than one hundred fuzzy objects observable with a small telescope. As it turned out, Messier's fuzzy objects are not comets. But comet sweepers have to eliminate known nebulae from consideration. If we're going to hunt comets, we need a copy of Messier's catalog. Then, we use the telescope to locate each of Meisser's fuzzies, and memorize its location. Once we're familiar with those common fuzzy objects, we're ready to hunt.

Comets are easier to see if they are close to the Sun. We begin a sweep by aiming the telescope at an area close to where the Sun went down. Then we scan a small area at a time, looking for fuzzy objects. If we find a fuzzy that we know is not in Messier's catalog, we'll check a star atlas and see if it identifies our fuzzy. If the object is not in current catalogs, it may be a comet.

Astronomers who think they have discovered a comet should contact the Central Bureau for Astronomical Telegrams.

*On January 30, 1996, using binoculars, Yuji Hyakutake discovered the brightest comet to visit the Earth in twenty years (top). Exactly one year later, Comet Hale-Bopp lit up the night sky (bottom). Thomas Bopp, Arizona, and Alan Hale, New Mexico, discovered the comet, the farthest one ever discovered by amateurs.*

1787

King George III gives Caroline Herschel a salary. William Herschel marries Mary Pitt.

# "Letter from Caroline Herschel (1750-1848)"

## A Poem by Siv Cedering

(In this poem the poet imagines herself as Caroline Herschel)

William is away, and I am minding
the heavens. I have discovered
eight new comets and three nebulae
never before seen by man,
and I am preparing an Index to
Flamsteed's observations, together with
a catalog of 560 stars omitted from
the British Catalog, plus a list of errata
in that publication. William says
I have a way with numbers, so I handle
the necessary reductions and
calculations. I also plan
every night's observation
schedule, for he says my intuition
helps me turn the telescope to discover
star cluster after star cluster.

I have helped him polish the mirrors
and lenses of our new telescope. It is
the largest in existence. Can you imagine
the thrill of turning it to some new
corner of the heavens to see
something never before seen
from earth? I actually like

that he is busy with the Royal Society
and his club, for when I finish my other work
I can spend all night sweeping
the heavens.

Sometimes when I am alone
in the dark, and the universe reveals
yet another secret, I say the names
of my long, lost sisters, forgotten
in the books that record
our science—
    Aganice of Thessaly,
    Hypatia,
    Hildegard,
    Catherina Hevelius,
    Maria Agnesi
—as if the stars themselves could remember.
Did you know that Hildegard
proposed a heliocentric universe
300 years before Copernicus? That she
wrote of universal gravitation 500 years
before Newton? But who would listen
to her? She was just a nun, a woman.
What is our age, if that age was dark?

1818

Maria Mitchell is born in Nantucket.

1823

Caroline Herschel returns to Germany after William's death.

As for my name, it will also be
forgotten, but I am not accused
of being a sorceress, like Aganice,
and the Christians do not threaten to
drag me to church, to murder me, like they did
Hypatia of Alexandria, the eloquent young
woman who devised the instruments
used to accurately measure the position
and motion of heavenly bodies.
However long we live, life is short, so I
work. And however important man becomes
he is nothing compared to the stars.
There are secrets, dear sister, and it is
for us to reveal them. Your name, like mine,
is a song. Write soon.

Caroline

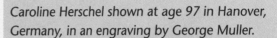

*Caroline Herschel shown at age 97 in Hanover, Germany, in an engraving by George Muller.*

When William died in 1822,
Caroline returned to Hanover to live
with her younger brother Dietrich.
She was now the foremost woman
astronomer in Europe. Astronomers
from all over visited her. The King of
Prussia awarded her the Gold Medal
of Science. And in 1835, when she was
eighty-two, the Royal Astronomical Society of England elected her
to honorary membership. Honor and recognition had finally come
to Caroline Herschel, along with her independence. The unpaid
household servant had become the First Lady of Comets. ◉

## 1835

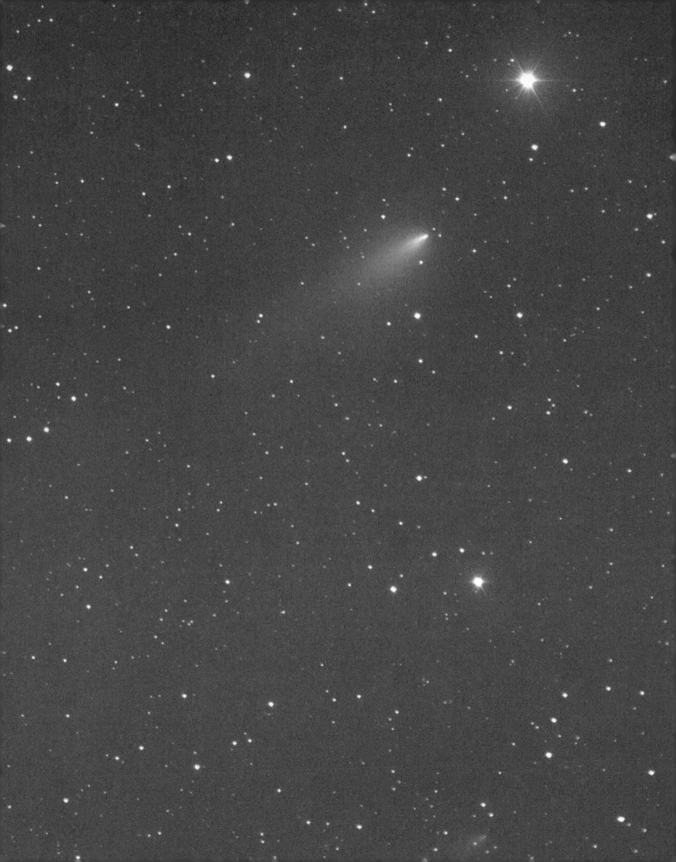

# Astronomy in the New World

In the early part of the nineteenth century, European astronomers swept the heavens with larger telescopes and catalogued more comets and nebulae. Across the Atlantic, American astronomers often used their skill to aid sailors and land surveyors. Even as a child, Maria Mitchell took responsibility for the safety of whalers who put out from Nantucket.

*A mathematical formula is a hymn of the Universe.*

Maria Mitchell

Twelve-year old Maria Mitchell buttoned the wool greatcoat to her chin and pulled up the hood. After lighting her whale-oil lamp, she picked up the telescope, metronome, and chronometer, and climbed the rough ladder-like stairs to the roof. Tonight was the most important night in her life.

# MARIA MITCHELL

*pronounced Mah-RYE-ah*

**born 1818**

**died 1889**

Her father was away, and for the first time she was going to rate a chronometer by herself. She took a deep breath as she began the painstaking process of rating a chronometer. She knew she could do the work. But she also knew the lives of Captain Chadwick and the crew of the whaler *Baltic* depended on her accuracy.

Maria blew on her icy fingers, set the metronome ticking, and focused the telescope on the first star she would use this night. As the metronome ticked off the seconds, Maria compared the time it took for the star to move a specific distance, to the time recorded by the chronometer. The next day, she delivered

## Maria Rates a Chronometer

From the time she was a small child, Maria Mitchell helped her father rate chronometers. With him at her side, she learned to identify a star, start the metronome ticking off seconds, and check the chronometer. Then she would follow the star across a fixed distance of the sky. If the seconds counted off by the metronome did not equal the seconds as measured by the chronometer, Maria would note the difference as a correction to the chronometer.

To double or triple check, Maria would choose another star and repeat the process. Because she understood that accurate timekeeping could save sailors' lives, she sometimes spent an entire night making sure her correction was right.

the chronometer to Captain Chadwick, who called her correction perfect.

When Maria Mitchell was born on the island of Nantucket, off the coast of Massachusetts, the island was the greatest whaling port in the world. The harbor could berth 125 ships and provide supplies for whalers from around the continent.

Most families in Nantucket either fished or whaled, and they were keenly aware of both the daytime and nighttime skies. The phases of the moon predicted the tides — ships entered port with the rising tide and sailed again with the outgoing tide. Sailors navigated by the stars and the sun. A sextant, a device for finding the angle between a star and the horizon, had a place in almost every house.

Rating chronometers was just one of the astronomical activities Maria and her father shared. Every clear night, she outfitted herself in the heavy winter clothing she called her regimentals, climbed to the widow's walk, a fenced deck on the roof, and set up her telescope. Sometimes she and her father tracked stars and confirmed previous observations. Sometimes they rated chronometers. And sometimes they swept the sky for comets.

She studied the stars with the same devotion that Caroline Herschel had. In the winter, in England, Caroline melted her frozen ink over a candle flame.

# Celestial Navigation

If we imagine ourselves in the middle of an ocean, facing endless water in every direction, we can understand the plight of sailors before the age of global positioning satellites. How would they know where they were?

Many centuries ago, navigators had learned to figure out their ship's north-south position, or latitude, using the location of the Sun, Moon, or stars, and the length of the day. Figuring out the ship's longitude, or east-west location, was more complicated. To locate the ship's longitude, sailors had to know the exact time on ship and the exact time at a place of known longitude, usually their home port.

To keep track of time in two locations, every ship carried two clocks, one set to home-port time, and one to ship's time. Each day, the navigator reset the ship's clock to 12:00 noon at the exact moment the Sun was at its highest point in the sky. The navigator could then convert the time difference between the two clocks to a distance in miles, using a conversion based on the ship's latitude.

Until the end of the eighteenth century, however, clocks on ships were not reliable. Metal parts expanded and contracted with temperature changes. Salt air, constant dampness, and rolling ships magnified the errors in ship-board time. The inability to know the precise time produced enormous errors in navigation. In 1707, two thousand English sailors drowned when a British fleet ran upon a jagged headland near Lands End in England. An error in navigation, caused by inaccurate time keeping, had led the sailors to believe they were sailing through the fog into a harbor, when they were actually headed straight onto the jagged rocks.

By Maria Mitchell's day, extremely accurate clocks, called chronometers, had nearly eliminated tragic navigation errors. To maintain the accuracy of his chronometer, every captain had his chronometer rated, or checked against the motion of the stars, in each port. Any discrepancy between celestial time and the chronometer was recorded as a correction. The captain would then apply this correction to the time reading every time he calculated his ship's position.

*After her mother's death, Maria assumed the care of her father.*
*Their mutual love of astronomy added to the bond between them.*
*This photo was taken at their cottage on the Vassar campus.*

Many houses in Nantucket were built with widow's walks, or porches, on the roof. High enough for people to study the sky and stars, or watch for ships at sea, the porches were called widow's walks because women often kept watch for husbands who had already disappeared at sea.

Maria Mitchell, in Nantucket, shoveled the snow off the widow's walk and relit the lamps that blew out. She brushed the frost off her notebook and continued peering through the telescope, counting seconds, and recording star positions in her journal.

When it was too foggy to see the stars, Maria tucked herself into the tiny, closet-like space that held her desk and taught herself mathematics and astronomy. One of the books she used, *The Study of Natural Philosophy*, was written by Caroline Herschel's brother William.

As Quakers, Maria's parents believed that all children should be educated, and their children went as far in school as possible. For the curious young Maria, Nantucket Island was even better than school. She wanted to know about everything and wandered the island collecting flowers, seashells, and driftwood. She stowed her treasures in the attic space, along with her telescope.

When she finished school at sixteen, Maria opened a school for girls as a way to help out the family finances. With ten children to support, her father's income was stretched thin, even after he became an officer in the Pacific Bank of Nantucket.

On the day her school opened, a September morning in 1835, Maria felt sick with fear that she would fail. What did she know about running a school or teaching? Maybe nobody would come. Finally, one girl, then another, appeared at the school door. By the time her students had settled down, Maria saw that among the white and Portuguese students, a few black girls had crept in cautiously. They feared they would be thrown out, since other schools in Nantucket did not allow black children to attend. But Maria welcomed them all, and her school filled rapidly.

Maria's school reflected her independence and progressive thinking. Her acceptance of all children was just one example of her independent streak. She had older children teach younger ones and took the children outside to study nature. Both students and parents were happy with the new school, but when a new opportunity appeared, Maria closed her school just a year after it opened.

In 1836, the City of Nantucket built a new library, called the Atheneum. The city offered eighteen-year-old Maria the position of librarian, and she eagerly accepted. The library was open to the public only in the afternoons. In the mornings, she had the entire library to herself. During those wonderful, solitary mornings, she taught herself German, physics, mathematics, and navigation.

The family fortunes improved quickly. Maria had a good position, and William Mitchell had a better-paying job as an officer at the Pacific Bank of Nantucket. The family moved to a bigger house attached to the bank building. Maria's father built a small observatory on the roof.

Maria's advertisement in the Nantucket newspaper read:

*Maria Mitchell proposes to open a school for girls on the first of next month at the Franklin School House. Instruction will be given in Reading, Spelling, Geography, Grammar, History, Natural Philosophy, Arithmetic, Geometry and Algebra. Terms: $3 per quarter. None admitted under six years of age.*

## 1848

## Products from Whales

Before scientists discovered the process for refining crude oil into gasoline and other useful products, people in America and Europe used whale oil in lamps, streetlights, and lanterns. They made bustles and hoop-skirts from whale bone, and umbrellas and buggy whips from whale baleen. The whaling center in Nantucket was so busy that a newspaper journalist reported seeing ninety ships in the harbor at one time. Sadly, some whales were hunted almost to extinction in a short time.

With the new observatory came new equipment, some on loan from West Point Academy, and some from the U. S. Coast Survey. William had done work for the Coast Survey for some time, and now they hired Maria to help her father survey the island of Nantucket. Along with making astronomical observations and doing calculations, Maria waded through swamps, slid down sand dunes, and climbed trees to sight markers. Her small salary from the Coast Survey allowed her to buy more books and equipment.

Maria's life settled into a comfortable routine. In the mornings, she studied and read; in the afternoons, she ran the library. And in the evenings, she and her father studied the stars from their new observatory.

Then, late in the evening on the night of October 1, 1847, Maria noticed a fuzzy object where she had seen nothing the night before. With growing excitement, she watched the object. Could it be a comet? She quickly checked the star catalogs and realized this was indeed a new, unreported comet.

Maria dashed down the stairs to where her parents were entertaining guests at dinner. She dragged her father to the roof and he confirmed her find. Sixty-one years after Caroline Herschel spotted her first comet in England, Maria Mitchell, born far across the Atlantic in the United States, became America's First Lady of Comets. Her discovery launched her public career as an astronomer and teacher, and made her the best known American woman scientist of her generation.

1853
Mitchell receives the Medal of Merit from Switzerland.

1857
Williamina Paton Stevens is born in Dundee, Scotland.

Chinese astronomers first recorded a visit from Halley's Comet in 240 BCE. Since then, every 76 to 79 years, the comet has revisited Earth, due to arrive again in 2062.

Maria's routine changed on that night in October. After he confirmed that she had found a comet, William Mitchell wrote immediately to professional astronomer friends at Cambridge University in Boston. He knew a comet spotter must lay quick claim to being the first to see a new comet. Mitchell's letter allowed their astronomer friends in Boston to confirm her sighting, and established that Maria was the first American to spot a new comet and the first astronomer in the world to report seeing this one.

The King of Denmark awarded Maria a gold medal for being the first person to spot this comet. Several other astronomers insisted they had seen this one first, but, thanks to her father's quick action in having other astronomers confirm her sighting, the king decided in Maria's favor.

Maria Mitchell's discovery of a comet, and the publicity that followed the award of the gold medal, turned the shy, retiring librarian into a celebrity. She was featured in the journal *Recent Progress in Astronomy,* and newspapers everywhere ran stories about her. Astronomers and scientists from around the world wrote to the Mitchells and visited them. A group of women presented

### *Mary Margaret Lindsay Murray Huggins*

was a musician, painter, and writer. Taught astronomy by her grandfather, she married William Huggins, a spectroscopist, in 1875. Together they produced some of the earliest stellar spectra. As a good friend of Sarah Whiting, director of the Wellesley College Observatory, Huggins left many of her astronomical instruments, as well as her notebooks and those of William, to Wellesley when she died.

1859

Gustav Kirchoff uses spectroscopy to identify the chemical elements in the Sun.

Maria with a telescope in recognition of her comet discovery and her increasing reputation as an astronomer.

Maria and her father began to travel more, to meet with their astronomy colleagues all over the world. And, in 1857, Maria sailed to Europe to meet astronomers and scientists, including John Herschel, Caroline Herschel's nephew. She particularly enjoyed her visit with Mary Somerville, the English mathematician and astronomer. Maria wrote in her journal that they talked of astronomy, new discoveries in chemistry, and the discovery of gold in California. Mrs. Somerville, she wrote, "was much interested in the photography of the stars and said that it had never been done in Europe."

Maria's mother died in 1861. Maria had nursed her through a long illness and now felt at loose ends. Most of her brothers and sisters had moved to the mainland. Nantucket was far away from both family and astronomy friends. Soon Maria moved with her father to Lynn, Massachusetts, to be close to her favorite sister, Kate. She set up her telescope and looked forward to a quiet life, observing stars and writing papers on astronomy. The universe, however, had other plans for Maria Mitchell.

Matthew Vassar, a wealthy philanthropist, had decided to build a women's college that would be the equal of the best men's colleges in America. He asked Maria to teach astronomy and to operate the college observatory.

***Nicole-Reine Lepaute***, wife of a French clock maker, studied the oscillations of pendulums of various lengths. Her understanding of pendulum behavior allowed her to excel in calculating the time of planetary rotations. She was known as one of the best astronomical computers of the day. The director of the Paris Observatory asked her for assistance in calculating the time of the return of Halley's comet.

***Wilhelmine Bottcher Witte*** and her daughter Minna constructed a model of the moon. They drew on it the details they had observed using their own telescope. In 1847, she became the first person in Germany to sight the comet discovered by Maria Mitchell.

***Caterina Scarpellini*** studied astronomy under the guidance of her uncle and compiled the first Italian catalog of meteors. She discovered a comet in 1854.

Maria hesitated. She had not attended college and felt she knew nothing about teaching in a college. She knew very little about the social rituals in vogue on the mainland, and she disliked fancy clothing and fancy manners. Her Nantucket childhood left her with a stubborn streak of independence. With husbands, sons, and fathers away whaling, many women on Nantucket ran their homes, their farms, and their businesses single-handedly. Maria's attitudes came from some of the most independent women in America.

Maria wasn't the only one who had reservations about women's colleges and women professors. Public figures and journalists all over America ranted against educating women. "You cannot feed a woman's brain without starving her body," declared one Dr. Edward Clarke. Some men insisted that educating women made them unfit mothers.

Other equally vocal men supported educating women. "There is no science which a man can learn that is impossible or improper for a woman," said Dr. Alexander Wilder. He pointed to Maria Mitchell as an example of a woman who, "though highly cultivated [educated] still has great vitality."

For Maria, a chance to work with the third largest telescope in the country was too much to resist, and she took the position. Maria, her father — and her cat — moved into the small house attached to the observatory of the new college. Then, on September 20, 1865, Vassar Female College, in Poughkeepsie, New York, opened its doors.

Maria was as nervous on her first day at Vassar as she had been when she opened her school on Nantucket. How would students respond to a lecture in a science most of them knew

***Louise Elisabeth du Piery*** calculated the lunar eclipses used by French astronomers to study lunar motion. She computed and published a variety of astronomical tables.

***Marie-Jeanne de Lalande*** lectured on astronomy in Paris. She named her daughter Caroline, after Caroline Herschel.

1865

Mitchell joins the American Philosophical Society. Vassar College for Women opens; Mitchell begins teaching there.

little about? Again, she needn't have worried. After a painful silence at the end of her lecture, one student said in surprise, "Why Miss Mitchell, I had always thought science dull. You have not made it so."

Maria's students loved her, but she struggled to settle in at Vassar. She hated the emphasis on appearances there. She grew up admiring the plain-spoken, plainly dressed, independent women of Nantucket. Her mother taught her to value honesty above all, and her Quaker background taught her to question authority and figure out why things were the way they were. She cared about what went on in students' heads, not what went on their backs.

Above all, she resisted the domination of the Lady Principal who set rules for the behavior of students and staff. She thought the Lady Principal's rules suggested that women needed to be taken care of.

She even defied the president of Vassar when he asked her not to sit in the window to mend her stockings on Sundays. The Sabbath was a day of rest, and he thought it set a bad example for students to see Maria working. In response, Maria moved her chair closer to the window.

Maria Mitchell had her own ideas about classroom conduct, too. She refused to take roll in her classes and resisted the standard grading system. She wanted to give all her students an "A." She said the brilliant and faithful girls deserved it. Bright but lazy girls should have an "A" because she admired their impudence, and dull girls should have an "A" to console them.

Although she fought the grading system, Maria let nothing stand in the way of her students' education.

## Rules from the Lady Principal

- Young ladies must not cross their ankles or sit sideways on a chair.

- A lady must not make a horseshoe when biting into a piece of bread.

- If a lady student writes to anyone other than a family member, the letter must be submitted to the Lady Principal for approval.

- Ladies must take two baths a week, no more, no less.

- Ladies must not leave the campus without an escort.

- Ladies must not appear at supper in the same dress they have worn during the day.

- Ladies must wear silk at dinner.

1866

Antonia Maury is born in Cold Spring, New York.

1868

Henrietta Swann Leavitt is born in Cambridge, Massachusetts.

When an apple tree blocked their view of a comet, she called the handy man and ordered him to chop the tree down. She defied a campus curfew, rousing her students out of bed at 3:00 o'clock in the morning to watch a lunar eclipse. And, twice she took students to distant places to watch eclipses of the Sun. Once they traveled to Colorado by train where, one student wrote to her parents, they were surrounded by rough-looking men with guns.

*Mitchell and her class at Vassar in about 1878.*

By today's standards, we would call Maria Mitchell a hard teacher. She might not want to give grades, but she insisted on nearly perfect work from her students. Her students were happy to accept her standards because she obviously loved astronomy and wanted her students to share her enthusiasm. One student, Ellen Swallow, who became a renowned chemist, wrote in her diary about her excitement when she made a discovery. "Found 2 star clusters Maria Mitchell did not know. She was greatly pleased and said to me, 'Do not spend any money on knickknacks. You will make valuable discoveries in your life.'" Later Ellen wrote, "I shall save money in all that I can, for I want a telescope more than anything else."

*Mitchell (seated at far left) and her students near Denver, Colorado, on July 29, 1878, observing a total solar eclipse.*

Throughout her life, Maria Mitchell fought for the equal education of women. "I believe in women even more than I

1873

Mitchell and student Mary W. Whitney in the Vassar observatory around 1877. Whitney became director of the observatory when Mitchell retired. She later went to Wellesley.

believe in astronomy," she wrote. She carried her passion for educating women equally into politics. She was active in the women's suffrage movement, the movement to allow women to vote. In 1873, she founded the Association for the Advancement of Women to promote better education for women, and she served as the first head of its science committee.

Maria Mitchell was not simply the first American to discover a comet. She had other astronomical interests as well: sunspots and solar eclipses. She took photographs of the Sun every day that it was visible for her entire adult life, and she studied the surfaces of Jupiter and Saturn.

She published papers on astronomy in all the important science journals of her day. She was elected to the American Academy of Arts and Sciences, the only woman member for more than fifty years. She was also the first woman elected to membership in the American Philosophical Society.

After her death, Vassar College erected a statue to Maria Mitchell, a tribute to its first astronomy teacher, and an acknowledgement of her skill in opening the eyes of her students to the wonders of the universe. She would take pride in knowing that twenty-five of her students went on to science careers so successful they were listed in *Who's Who in America*.

As additional tribute, her friends and colleagues founded the Maria Mitchell Association on Nantucket in 1902, specifically to encourage young women to study astronomy. ◉

1875

# Human Computers Before Silicon Chips

Today the word "computer" brings to mind Macs and PCs. In the first two decades of the twentieth century, however, an employer who advertised for a computer was looking for a person to do calculations. From 1880 until the invention of electronic computers, astronomical observatories hired many such human computers. Harvard Observatory and the U.S. Naval Observatory employed the greatest number of women. Mina Fleming was the first female computer at Harvard Observatory.

*An achievement bordering on the marvelous.*

*A colleague*

# WILLIAMINA PATON STEVENS FLEMING

**born 1857**

**died 1911**

My Scottish maid could do a better job than you're doing." In 1881, Professor Edward Pickering of the Harvard Observatory lost his temper over the mistakes his young male assistant kept making. To prove his point, Pickering brought his maid into the observatory and taught her to do the assistant's work. She did more than prove his point. Mina Fleming, Professor Pickering's Scottish housekeeper, became the founding mother of the women computers of Harvard and the first female astrophysicist.

**Ida Barney** did most of the computations for the thirteen-volume *Yale Photographic Zone Catalogue* of star positions. The catalog required a half million measurements and twenty-three years of work.

Mina Stevens had been an outstanding student in her native Dundee, Scotland. At fourteen, she tutored other students in math, science, and languages. At nineteen, Mina married, added Fleming to her name, and sailed across the Atlantic Ocean with her husband, to Boston.

The marriage was stormy, and her husband deserted her while she was pregnant. She then took the unheard-of step of divorcing him. To support herself and her baby, Mina turned to the only employment then available to most women, housekeeping. Luckily, her new employer was Professor Pickering. Soon she was working at the Harvard Observatory.

Mina Fleming had no training in either astronomy or spectroscopy, but she was always a good student. She easily learned how to scan photographic plates and calculate wavelengths. And with her quick mind and good eyes, she swiftly recognized differences in spectra. As she began to see patterns in the spectra she studied, she developed a new way to classify stars by their spectral patterns. She and Pickering realized the classifications corresponded to the brightness of the stars.

In her first ten years at Harvard, Fleming classified more than ten thousand stars. She recorded her work in a catalog published in 1890, *The Pickering-Fleming System of Stellar Classification*. This catalog is still used by astronomers today.

One group of stars Fleming identified early on she called variable stars. Variable stars change brightness over a fixed period of time. Fleming published studies of more than two hundred variable stars. One scientist who reviewed her work wrote, "Many astronomers are deservedly proud to have discovered one variable and content to leave the arrangements for its observation to others; the discovery of 222, and the care of their future on this scale, is an achievement bordering on the marvelous."

Fleming was a capable administrator as well as a talented astronomer. During her time at Harvard, she trained nearly fifty young women hired by the Observatory to do computations on stellar spectra. She organized their work and scheduled their daily activities, proofread their calculations and checked their stellar classifications.

Although Fleming's administrative duties left her less time for astronomy, Pickering recognized her service in both areas. In 1898, he appointed her Curator of Astronomical Photographs. She was the first woman appointed to such a position at Harvard University.

Professor Pickering was probably delighted that he had the foresight to hire women for the painstaking and tedious work of

The women's workroom at Harvard Observatory. Antonia Maury is seated third from left, and Mina Fleming is standing at center.

Eleanor A. Lamson, left, and Etta M. Eaton, work in the computation room at the U.S. Naval Observatory in this 1903 photograph.

astronomical computations. However, his attitude toward women in general was not much more enlightened than that of many men of his time. Mina Fleming wrote in her diary:

> During the morning's work on correspondence etc. I had some conversation with the Director [Pickering] regarding women's salaries. He seems to think that no work is too much or too hard for me, no matter what the responsibility or how long the hours. But let me raise the question of salary and I am immediately told that I receive an excellent salary as women's salaries stand.

Pickering may not have fully appreciated Fleming's skills and dedication, but other astronomers were quite impressed by her achievements. Her peers elected her the first American woman member of the Royal Astronomical Society. In 1907, she published her study of the 222 variable stars she had discovered. Before her death in 1911, she published her discovery of white dwarf stars, those that appear to be collapsing in on themselves. Her work provided a foundation on which future astronomers would build their understanding of stellar processes. ◉

*Mary Whitney*, a student of Maria Mitchell's, succeeded her as professor of astronomy and director of the Vassar Observatory in 1888. Her study focused on double stars, variable stars, asteroids, comets, and the precise measurement of photographic plates. She helped numerous women find jobs as astronomers.

1876

Fleming moves to Boston at age nineteen.

1881

Fleming begins work at Harvard Observatory.

# The Electromagnetic Spectrum

*Star light, star bright, first star I see tonight ...*

The light we see when we pick out a star to wish on is just a tiny bit of the total amount of radiation the star is emitting. Stars give off much more radiation than the visible light our eyes detect. The whole range, called the electromagnetic spectrum, runs between short wavelength radiation, such as X-rays, and long wavelength radiation, such as radio waves and microwaves.

Human beings are not very good detectors of electromagnetic radiation. If a star is relatively close to us, as our Sun is, we feel its infrared radiation as heat. Our eyes see only the wavelengths we call light, and our skin tans or burns from ultraviolet radiation. We don't consciously detect any of the rest of the radiation emitted by a star, and some of it doesn't even penetrate our atmosphere. Astronomers use specifically designed instruments to study the long wavelength or short wavelength emissions of stars.

Early study of stellar spectra focused on visible light. The radio waves and X-rays emitted by stars were not discovered until the second half of the twentieth century. Instruments that detect radio waves, microwaves, and X-rays now allow astronomers to study stars over the entire range of the electromagnetic spectrum.

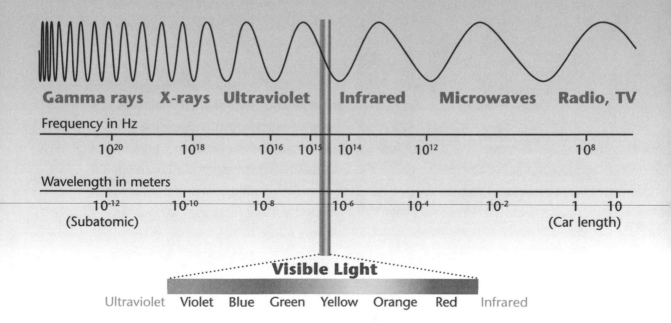

**Gamma rays    X-rays    Ultraviolet    Infrared    Microwaves    Radio, TV**

Frequency in Hz

$10^{20}$        $10^{18}$        $10^{16}$    $10^{15}$  $10^{14}$        $10^{12}$                $10^{8}$

Wavelength in meters

$10^{-12}$        $10^{-10}$        $10^{-8}$        $10^{-6}$        $10^{-4}$        $10^{-2}$        $1$        $10$
(Subatomic)                                                                                (Car length)

**Visible Light**

Ultraviolet    Violet    Blue    Green    Yellow    Orange    Red    Infrared

## The Cost of Computers in 1875

In Cambridge, Massachusetts, in the late nineteenth century, about half the women who worked outside the home worked as maids, cooks, and laundry workers. The other half worked in cotton mills. These jobs all required little formal education but demanded hard physical labor and long hours. They also paid very little. Women with college degrees preferred to work as computers at the Harvard Observatory, as well as at other observatories. Their work was not physically hard, the environment was pleasant, and the pay was better than they would get at other jobs.

Women computers at Harvard worked seven hours a day, every day but Sunday, and earned $546 a year, far less than male astronomers doing the same job. The men were paid about $800 per year. Even male salesclerks made at least $780 a year.

The difference in salaries between men and women was based on their gender rather than their ability. Edward Pickering wrote in a report in 1898 that women were "capable of doing as much good routine work as astronomers who would receive larger salaries. Three or four times as many [female] assistants can be employed." Even in the twenty-first century, the effort to require that men and women be paid equivalent salaries for work of equivalent value faces opposition.

These days, the salaries of male and female astronomers is closer than in many jobs. And every junior high school student with an electronic calculator has more calculating power at her fingertips than Professor Pickering had with a room full of computers.

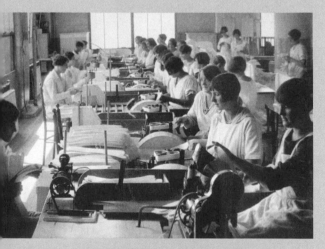

Women factory workers folding and ironing linen collars.

1887

Maury graduates from Vassar.

1888

Mitchell retires from Vassar. Maury begins work at Harvard Observatory.

By 1930, Harvard College Observatory led the world in stellar photography, wavelength computations, and the employment of women astronomers. Few of these women had studied astronomy formally and none held doctorates. However, from 1880 through 1940, women provided the computational power that drove astronomical research. One of those women was Annie Cannon.

*...recognized the world over as the greatest living expert in this line of work.*

A European astronomer

# ANNIE JUMP CANNON

**born 1863**

**died 1941**

Follow my finger, Annie," her mother said. "Down the bowl, across, and up the handle. Do you see the dipper? That's what we call it. The Greeks named it Ursa Major, the Great Bear."

As she watched her mother point out and name the constellations in the night sky, Annie Cannon realized she was a very lucky little girl. While her friends squinted over cross-stitch samplers and pricked themselves with sharp needles, Annie watched stars with her mother. And now, the post had delivered a brand new telescope. Annie and her

**Alice Mabel Gray**
earned a degree in
mathematics from the
University of Chicago
and worked at the U.S.
Naval Observatory, where
she became known as
an eccentric. She cut her
hair short and worked in
pants. She later served as
editorial secretary for the
*Astrophysical Journal*, but
retired from public life at
thirty-five. A free spirit
and naturalist, she lived
in a shack on the shores
of Lake Michigan and
earned the little money
she needed by making
and selling driftwood
boxes. In 1925, she died
of kidney failure at
forty-three.

mother would be able to see the rings of Saturn. They might also see the double star in the handle of Ursa Major.

They set up the telescope in the attic. Here a big window gave Annie a good view of the night sky over Dover, Delaware. Her mother helped her haul a chair and a little table up the attic steps. Annie added a candle, pen, and a journal. And there she had it, her own personal observatory.

Annie's father encouraged her nightly observing and her recording of the movement of the stars and planets in her notebook. But he paced the floor below, worried that her candle would burn down the house. Still, he supported equal education for women. He was already thinking about which college Annie might attend.

The summer Annie turned sixteen, she watched her father ship a large box of peaches to the president of Wellesley College. Wilson Cannon, a Delaware Senator and experienced politician, knew how to ensure that Annie would be accepted to the college of his choice. With an outstanding astronomy program, Wellesley was Annie's choice, too.

Wellesley's astronomy professor, Mary Whitney, one of Maria Mitchell's former students, had built a first-rate astronomy program. It included classes in stellar spectroscopy, and Annie was fascinated by spectroscopy. She said it reminded her of the beautiful rainbows cast by cut-glass ornaments that hung from crystal candelabra in the family dining room.

While Annie loved Wellesley, the brutal New England winters came as a shock. Used to the warmer climate of Delaware, she had not packed the right clothes for Massachusetts. The first time she caught cold, she got an ear infection, and these infections recurred every winter. By

1889                    1890

Maria Mitchell dies.    Harvard Observatory publishes Fleming's stellar data. Cannon enters Wellesley's graduate program.

the time she graduated, her hearing was damaged. The problem got worse with time. Later in life she became completely deaf.

After graduating from Wellesley, Annie went back to her prosperous home in Dover. For the next ten years, she enjoyed her position as a popular young hostess. Life was full of parties, travel, and visits to friends.

An early fan of photography, Annie loved to take pictures of landmarks. She sent her photos to newspapers and magazines, where many of them were printed. Her growing reputation as a photographer led one camera company to publish photographs in a booklet that was sold as a souvenir at the 1893 World's Fair.

Annie was very close to her mother, and when she died suddenly, Annie was shattered. She could not bear the family home with its ghosts and memories. She returned to Wellesley in 1893 for graduate work in astronomy.

At thirty-three, Cannon completed her degree and went to work at the Harvard Observatory with Mina Fleming. She applied her photographic expertise to analyzing spectra and categorizing stars.

For the next forty years, Annie Cannon analyzed stellar spectra on photographic plates. She calculated wavelengths and placed each star in a category based on the pattern she saw in its spectrum. She labeled the categories A, B, C, and so on. Then she arranged her categories so they showed a smooth transition from one type into another. The sequence now became O, B, A, F, G, K, M. Then, for each major category, Cannon found sub-categories.

Astronomers soon realized the categories organized the stars by temperature, not by their composition. Our Sun is a G2 star, just about in the middle of the temperature range.

Cannon became so skilled at analyzing stellar spectra that she could spot peculiarities on photographic plates almost

O

B

A

F

G

K

M

Annie Cannon earns her masters' from Wellesley.

Maury publishes her new stellar classifications.

instantly. She would look at a photograph of a star's spectrum, immediately recognize the star's classification, and call it out to an assistant, who wrote it down. Cannon often classified more than three stars a minute.

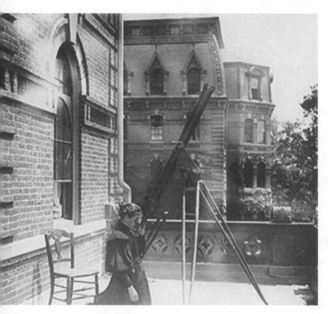

*Annie Cannon began graduate work in astronomy at Wellesley in 1893. She was especially interested in stellar spectra.*

Astronomer Cecilia Payne-Gaposchkin, who came to Harvard in 1920, was asked once how Cannon classified each spectral type so rapidly. Cecilia said she thought Annie would "not be able to tell them, because she didn't know herself. She did not think about the spectra as she classified them, she simply recognized them."

As she became increasingly deaf, Annie used the crude hearing aids then available. Several coworkers suspected that she turned down the volume when she wanted to concentrate in the busy, noisy lab. Despite her hearing loss, her friends described her as one of the happiest people they knew. She formed warm and lasting friendships, and wrote long letters to family, friends, classmates, and professional and amateur astronomers everywhere. She hosted parties for local children and her colleagues at the cozy home she called Star Cottage on the Harvard campus.

Despite her expertise and productivity, Annie Cannon's contributions were not officially recognized by Harvard University for years. Finally, in 1938, two years before her death, she was named a professor of astronomy at Harvard. Twenty-seven years earlier, a visiting committee of the observatory had reported, "It is an anomaly that, though she is recognized the

1900

Cecilia Payne is born in Wendover, England.

1905

Helen Sawyer is born in Lowell, Massachusetts.
Albert Einstein publishes his theory of special relativity.

## Stellar Spectroscopy Is Born

In the early 1880s, astronomers made a marvelous discovery. They found a way to identify the chemical elements present in stars, from our own Sun to points of light thousands of light years away.

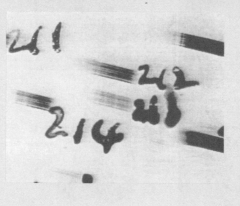

In 1872, Henry Draper produced the first stellar spectrogram. In his memory, Draper's widow endowed a stellar spectroscopy laboratory at the Harvard Observatory, where Mina Fleming went to work.

When sunlight passes through raindrops, it produces a circular spectrum of color: red, orange, yellow, green, blue, indigo, violet. We call this spectrum a rainbow. Unlike a rainbow, the spectrum from a star has dark lines superimposed over it, sort of a stellar bar code. The lines appear because the elements in the star absorb light at different wavelengths, literally sucking the light away at that wavelength.

Astronomers realized that the dark lines in spectra identify the chemical elements present in the star.

If an astronomer connects a telescope and prism to a camera, she can take a picture of a star's spectrum. This photograph, or spectrogram, creates a permanent record of the star's composition. Stellar spectroscopy is the science of creating and studying photographs of stellar spectra.

The women computers at Harvard calculated the wavelengths of the stars' light as recorded on the spectrograms. Then, they grouped stars in categories, called classes, according to their spectral patterns. They gave the classes letters of the alphabet for titles. Astronomers discovered later that the stellar classes developed by the women of Harvard actually grouped stars according to their temperatures and ages.

**1910**

Sawyer sees Halley's comet.

**1911**

Cannon becomes curator of photographs at Harvard Observatory. Mina Fleming dies.

*Cannon at work at the Harvard College Observatory. Cameras attached to telescopes recorded stellar spectra on glass plates. Cannon and her colleagues mounted the spectrograms in wood frames. They placed the frames near windows so that light came through the plate and illuminated the stars or the spectra they studied.*

*Annie Cannon and Henrietta Leavitt came to Harvard about the same time, and both suffered hearing loss, which may have added to their friendship.*

world over as the greatest living expert in this line of work . . . yet she holds no official position in the university."

Annie Jump Cannon made enormous contributions to astronomy, classifying the spectra of more than 350,000 stars. In 1900, when she took over the responsibility for the catalog on variable stars, it held just 14,000 entries. Forty years later, she had increased that number to a quarter of a million. She also discovered 300 variable stars and 500 novae, or exploding stars. ◉

1912

Vesto Slipher discovers stellar redshift.

For thousands of years, sky watchers wondered how far away the stars were. Henrietta Leavitt's discoveries gave astronomers a way to measure distances among stars.

*Possessing the best mind at the Observatory.*

A colleague of Leavitt's

# HENRIETTA SWAN LEAVITT

**born 1868**

**died 1921**

Henrietta Leavitt gazed intently at the glass plate supported in a wood frame. Below the plate, a mirror magnified and focused light from a nearby window. Every bit of light helped Leavitt with the task of comparing the size and location of the tiny black dots on this plate to those on other plates.

Like the other computers in the room, twenty-four-year-old Leavitt wore a dark, floor-length skirt. Today she had topped hers with a lace blouse, its jabot secured at her throat with a cameo brooch. Her dark hair lay in a sleek bun at the nape of her neck.

The plate Leavitt scanned was one of hundreds shipped from Harvard Observatory's outpost in Arequipa, Peru. Technicians in Peru photographed the stars in the Magellanic Clouds, bright star clusters visible only in the southern hemisphere. Then they sent boxes of plates to Harvard for analysis. On this day in 1904, Leavitt studied the stars in the Small Magellanic Cloud. She looked at plates taken at different times. As she flipped back and forth

between the new plates and those previously taken, she saw
something exciting. Several stars seemed to be different sizes at
different times. They appeared to grow, then shrink, then grow
again. The Small Magellanic Cloud was full of variable stars.

The more plates she studied, the more variable stars
she found. When her findings were published, a Princeton
astronomer wrote, "What a variable-star 'fiend' Miss Leavitt is."
Her discovery would give astronomers a way to measure distances
between stars for the first time.

Henrietta Swann Leavitt was the oldest of seven children
born to the Reverend George Roswell Leavitt and his wife, also
named Henrietta. The Leavitts' comfortable finances and liberal
ideas allowed Henrietta to enroll in Oberlin College at age
seventeen.

Four years later, she took the rigorous entrance exams and
applied to Radcliffe in Cambridge. In the exams, Henrietta easily

*A few of the women astronomers at Harvard Observatory. The year is unknown, but dress styles were changing. The older the women, the longer the skirts. Henrietta Leavitt stands*

1913

The International Committee on Photographic Magnitudes adopts the Pickering-Leavitt standards for stellar magnitude.

translated passages from Latin, Greek, and German into English. She successfully solved problems in advanced algebra and geometry, as well as in physics and astronomy. Her only weakness was in literature, and she was allowed to retake the test during her first year. Henrietta did well at Radcliffe, and graduated just before her twenty-fourth birthday.

The first astronomy class she took at Radcliffe had intrigued Leavitt. After graduation, she volunteered to work at the Harvard Observatory, an arrangement that would let her earn graduate credits and learn more about astronomy. Happy to have another computer, particularly one he didn't even have to pay, Professor Pickering put her to work calculating the brightness of stars on photographic plates produced at Harvard and in Peru.

For two years, Leavitt analyzed plates and wrote reports of her findings. In 1896, she sailed to Europe, where she traveled for two years. Then, instead of returning to Harvard, she went to live

**1915**
Albert Einstein publishes his theory of general relativity.

**1917**
Payne wins scholarship to Cambridge.

**1918**
Maury returns to Harvard.

in Beloit, Wisconsin, where her family had moved.

During her time away from Harvard, Leavitt's eyes caused her problems. Her friends noticed her hearing was getting worse. She missed the work at Harvard, which she described in a letter as "work I undertook with such delight." In a letter, she asked Pickering if he could recommend an observatory where she could work in a milder winter climate. In his response, Pickering offered her a full-time job at thirty cents an hour, "although our usual price, in such cases, is twenty-five cents an hour." Leavitt decided to take the job, even with the cold winters. And finally, in August, she was back in Cambridge to stay, ready to concentrate on the Magellanic Clouds.

Six years after returning to the hunt for variable stars, Leavitt published her report, *1777 Variables in the Magellanic Clouds.*

The report was a blockbuster in science circles because of the great number of variable stars Leavitt had categorized. The real breakthrough, however, came at the end of the report. Here she wrote, "It is worthy of notice that the brighter variables have the longer periods." That sentence, almost an aside, described one of the decade's most significant discoveries.

*Henrietta Leavitt at work calculating stellar magnitudes, possibly on stars of the Magellanic Clouds.*

Leavitt had discovered that a star's magnitude, or brightness, could be judged from the rate at which it dimmed and brightened. Astronomers understood immediately that if they knew how fast a star pulsed, they could estimate its relative brightness. And, if they could estimate the relative brightness of these stars, they could calculate relative distances between

## 1919

variable stars. If Leavitt was right, astronomers now had a way to estimate distances among stars for the first time. They could also make the first estimates of the size of our own Milky Way galaxy.

Before she could savor her success, however, Leavitt became very ill. Just before Christmas, she was hospitalized in Boston. Released from the hospital, she returned to her family in Beloit to recover.

Neither Leavitt nor Pickering was happy about her absence from the observatory. With the help of Mina Fleming, they worked out a way for Leavitt to work in Beloit. Fleming shipped Leavitt a box full of plates, an eyepiece, and a viewing frame. Once again, she could set the wood frame on a table near a window, insert the six-by-six-inch glass plates into the frame above a mirror, and begin comparing sizes and locations of the stars that appeared as black spots on the plates. She wrote back that she was able to work two or three hours a day.

Leavitt did not return to Harvard until 1910, and then for just a short time. Her father died suddenly, and she went back to Beloit to be with her mother. Along with consoling her mother, Leavitt struggled with her increasing hearing loss. Eventually she would become almost completely deaf.

Unwilling to let Leavitt's research lapse completely, Pickering again shipped her a box of plates. And again she was able to send him a report on her work. This time she had enough data to do a careful analysis of the relationship between the period of a variable star (the rate at which it pulses) and its magnitude. Now she confirmed that the pulse rate was directly related to the

### Ellen Barndollar
studied planet perturbations at the University of California. She was known for performing all calculations in duplicate.

### Dorothy Klumpke
earned her PhD from the Sorbonne in 1893. She could not find a research job and was hired to direct the female computation staff at the Paris Observatory.

### Margaretta Palmer
earned a PhD from Yale in 1894 and worked there on the computational staff.

**1920**

Harlow Shapley and Heber Curtis publicly debate the nature of nebulae.

**1921**

Henrietta Leavitt dies.

magnitude of the star in its brightest phase.

In 1912, the Harvard Observatory published a short paper proclaiming Leavitt's accomplishments. Her success did not lead to recognition as a true researcher, however. Professor Pickering refused to give her permission to take advanced classes that would have increased her theoretical understanding of the stars she studied. Despite the restrictions, she discovered more than 2400 variable stars, half of all those known in her day.

In 1913, she published her standard of photographic measurement, called *The Harvard Standard*. Leavitt's method for comparing stellar magnitude was used until the mid-1940s.

One of Leavitt's colleagues at the observatory said she "possessed the best mind at the observatory." In her autobiography, Cecilia Payne-Gaposchkin called Pickering's restrictions on Leavitt's study "a harsh decision which probably set back the study of variable stars for several decades, and condemned a brilliant woman to uncongenial work."

Henrietta Leavitt died at fifty-two from cancer, just before Professor Mittag-Leffler of the Swedish Academy of Science could nominate her for the Nobel Prize. The prizes are awarded only to living people. ◉

**Etta Maine Eaton** received her BA from Mt. Holyoke in 1889. In 1900, she became one of the first female computers at the Naval Observatory. She published observational information on comets in the *Astronomical Journal*.

**Eleanor Annie Lamson** received her MS in astronomy from George Washington University in 1899 and went to work at the Naval Observatory in 1900. She supervised all aspects of an expedition to Martha's Vineyard in 1925 to photograph a solar eclipse.

---

**1922**

Cannon discovers a nova.

**1923**

Payne enters Radcliffe and begins to work at the Harvard Observatory.

## Cepheid Variables and Stellar Distances

Variable stars pulsate, expanding and contracting as they grow brighter and dimmer. The Cepheid variables are very bright, giant stars that can be seen at great distances. Some of the first variables discovered, Cepheids vary between spectral types F and G as they pulsate. Their periods range from three days to fifty days, and their magnitude changes by as much as twenty times.

**F**

**G**

By 1900, astronomers could measure the distance from Earth to the closest star. But the process they used didn't work when objects were more than five light years away from Earth, or from each other. Astronomers needed a different way to measure distances to the rest of the objects they could see.

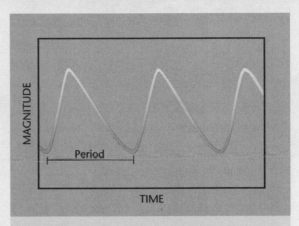

*The graph shows a variable star's rapid increase in brightness, then a slow dimming. Periods of variable stars range from several hours to several days. The brightening and dimming also makes the star appear to change in size, growing larger as it becomes brighter and shrinking as it dims.*

In 1912, Henrietta Leavitt discovered that stars that blink at the same rate have the same ultimate brightness, called absolute magnitude. She also knew that the brightness of a light decreases according to the square of the distance that the light is away from the observer. For example, if star A and star B blink at the same rate,

they have the same absolute magnitude, or brightness. If star B appears to be half ($\frac{1}{2}$) as bright as star A, it must be four times as far from observers on Earth as star A. That is, $(\frac{1}{D})^2 = (\frac{1}{2})^2 = \frac{1}{4}$. Leavitt's discovery gave astronomers a way to determine the distance from Earth to distant stars, as well as between the stars themselves.

Competition among observatories began to heat up after 1850. Each new telescope was bigger and better than the last, and without new telescopes, Harvard Observatory could not compete in the race to see farther into the heavens. Edward Pickering believed that Harvard's reputation in astronomy would depend on the amount of data he could generate, not on theories about what those data meant. And he believed in the smart, dedicated women who could turn out enormous amounts of data. Antonia Maury expected to get credit for her work.

# ANTONIA CAETANA MAURY

**born 1866**

**died 1952**

*I worked out the theory at the cost of much effort . . .*

Antonia Maury

Antonia Maury picked up the glass plates, one by one, and held them up to the window. The new spectrograms were spectacular! Unlike the dark smudges on the plates she had worked from in Maria Mitchell's classes at Vassar, Maury could see many sharp, fine lines on the plates made on the new Harvard equipment. Twenty-one-year-old Antonia Maury knew these sharp lines would reveal new secrets about the stars, and she was just the person to tease out the meaning of this new stellar information.

Maury had grown up among astronomers and astronomy. Edward Pickering was a friend of her father's. Her Aunt Mary was the widow of Henry Draper, who had made the first photographs of stellar spectra. And Mary Draper's money had established the Stellar Spectroscopy laboratory at Harvard in her uncle Henry Draper's name.

As everyone expected, Antonia attended Vassar College. There she became a student of Maria Mitchell's and graduated with honors in 1887. With her family connections and a degree in astronomy, it was only natural that Maury would work at Harvard Observatory.

Professor Pickering assigned her the job of classifying (arranging by magnitude) the bright stars in the northern sky. When Maury saw the groups of close, sharp lines, she was sure the new spectrograms showed important new information about stars. She suggested changing the classifications to include the new information.

***Winnifred Edgerton*** was the first American woman to earn a doctorate in astronomy, in 1886, and the first woman to earn a degree from Columbia University. She was admitted with the proviso that her admission "established no precedent for others."

Professor Pickering insisted the new detail was not important and rejected her suggestions. He refused even to discuss possible changes to the classification system. Undaunted, Maury worked on her own time to develop a new system. She wanted to know why there were differences in the spectrograms. What did the new lines mean about stellar compositions, the chemical makeup of stars? And in particular, Maury wanted to know why one star, Beta Lyrae, produced different spectra at different times.

Her independence and strong-minded views created constant conflicts between her and Professor Pickering. Even her aunt Mary quarreled with her, supporting Pickering over her niece.

At the height of her disagreements with Pickering, Maury quit Harvard. For the next twenty years, she taught school and continued her research, using the facilities at Vassar. And, although he disparaged her efforts, Professor Pickering still wanted her to give him the notebooks she had begun at Harvard so someone else could continue the work. Maury wrote back:

> I do not think it is fair to myself that I should pass the work into other hands until it can stand as work done by me. I worked out the theory at the cost of much

thought and elaborate comparison and I think I should have full credit for my theory of the relations of the star spectra and also for my theories in regard to Beta Lyrae. Would it not be fair that I should, at whatever time the results are published, receive credit for whatever I leave in writing in regard to these matters?

Maury knew that Mina Fleming had received only a brief mention for the first *Draper Catalog,* despite the fact that she had done all the work. Maury was not willing to see her own efforts slighted in the same way. When she finally published her new classifications, other astronomers immediately recognized their importance. Danish astronomer Ejnar Hertzsprung realized that the information in Maury's catalog corresponded with some of his own findings.

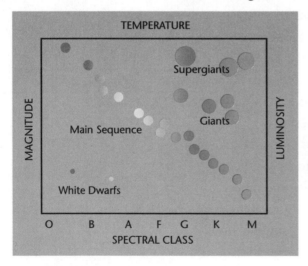

The Hertzsprung-Russell diagram.

Hertzsprung told Pickering that his refusal to recognize Maury's classifications was a bit like a zoologist detecting the difference between a whale and a fish, but continuing to call them both fish. Hertzsprung used Maury's classifications to help him create a diagram that grouped stars by their spectral class, size, and brightness. The diagram, called the Hertzsprung-Russell diagram, is a fundamental tool for astronomers. It allows them to study the way stars are born, evolve, and die.

Pickering and Maury finally settled their differences, and she returned to Harvard in 1918. Two years later, Harlow Shapley became director of the observatory. He recognized the importance of Maury's classifications and put them to use immediately.

Maury gained some recognition for her work and stayed

# The Beginning and End of Radcliffe

Women have been pounding on Harvard University's doors for generations. The oldest university in America opened in 1636. After a long wait, determined women scholars founded Radcliffe College and contracted with Harvard for instruction. In 1879 Harvard took on Radcliffe as its "annex" and essentially controlled it thereafter. Radcliffe admitted women and granted them degrees, keeping the Harvard culture overwhelmingly male.

Despite its lower status, Radcliffe graduated outstanding scholars and leaders, including Helen Keller, Elizabeth Holtzman (youngest U.S. Congresswoman), Benazir Bhutto (prime minister, Pakistan), and literary figures such as Gertrude Stein and Ursula K. Le Guin. Radcliffe women famously out-performed their male colleagues at Harvard, a fact one Harvard professor attributed in an article to "nothing more than dutiful drudgery." He meant the women weren't smarter; they just worked harder and were less sociable.

*Agassiz House at Radcliffe Yard.*

From the 1940s to the 70s, women students went from attending a separate college to attending Harvard's classes, activities, and housing. Radcliffe did not disappear in name, but many felt it vanish in practice. All the women's colleges, including Wellesley and Vassar, debated the continuation of separate education and the implications of co-education. After the 1970s, most had merged with men's colleges or become co-ed.

In 1999, the Harvard Corporation announced that Radcliffe College would cease to exist and instead become the Radcliffe Institute for Advanced Study, a center for the study of women, gender and society. Its Schlesinger Library is the nation's most important collection on women's history.

Harvard still lags behind other top universities in the promotion of women faculty. Change is still possible — on February 15, 2007, Harvard announced the appointment of Drew Gilpin Faust as the first female president of Harvard University.

## The Equal Rights Amendment

Proposed as an amendment to the U.S. Constitution in 1921, the Equal Rights Amendment states: "Equality of rights under the law shall not be denied or abridged by the United States or by any State on account of sex." For fifty years, the amendment was bottled up in committee and not released to the floor of either house for vote.

In 1971, the U.S. House of Representatives passed the amendment. On March 22, 1972, the U.S. Senate also passed the amendment and sent it to the states for ratification.

The amendment failed to gain ratification by the required number of states before the June, 1982, deadline. The amendment has been reintroduced into every session of Congress since 1982, but has never passed again.

at Harvard until her death in 1952. But she remained an outsider with no access to the real scientific work of the observatory. She could not take the advanced classes that would have extended her knowledge of astronomy, and she spent her time on routine and boring assignments. Payne-Gaposchkin wrote, "I remember Miss Maury saying to me, rather sadly, "I always wanted to learn the calculus but Professor Pickering didn't wish it."

## Women Astronomers, Wins and Losses

The discoveries the women at Harvard made while computing wavelengths and stellar classifications are of a quality that would have earned men in the same position numerous awards, even Nobel Prizes. The data collected and compiled by these women formed the basis for the next fifty years of astronomical research.

By the 1930s, women without doctorates found it harder to work as astronomers. At the same time, fewer universities admitted women to astronomy graduate programs. As a result, the number of women astronomers everywhere decreased rapidly.

Finally, in the early 1970s, the U.S. Congress passed equal rights legislation, Title IX, aimed specifically at education, that allowed women to study for advanced degrees in the sciences. ◉

# Rise of the Academics

By the end of the nineteenth century, some astronomers joked that American leadership in the field was due to two discoveries: George Hale discovered money and Edward Pickering discovered women. Hale raised money from newly wealthy U.S. citizens, such as industrialist Charles T. Yerkes, who financed construction of the Yerkes Observatory near Chicago. The main telescope at Yerkes, a forty-inch refractor, is still the largest refracting telescope in the world.

Edward Pickering hired the computing women at Harvard. They produced and organized the data that allowed astronomers to make sense of new discoveries and to advance theories that furthered our understanding of the universe.

*Harvard College Observatory in the early twentieth century.*

With the rise of big telescopes and other costly instruments, astronomy became an expensive, more competitive, and male-dominated science. The requirement of a PhD, combined with the difficulties women faced in obtaining such degrees, rapidly reduced the numbers of women in astronomy. Fortunately, a few women persevered and become professional astronomers. One of those, Cecilia Payne-Gaposchkin, has been called the most brilliant astronomer of her generation.

*The reward . . .*
*is the thrill of being the first*
*person in the history of the world*
*to see something.*

Cecilia Payne-Gaposchkin

# CECILIA
# PAYNE
# GAPOSCHKIN

**born 1900**

**died 1979**

Twelve-year-old Cecilia Payne was sure she was going to die. Uprooted from her cherished home in the lovely green village of Wendover, England, she'd been transplanted to the grimy streets of London. And in place of her local school, where she had greeted each day with excitement and delight, here she sat in a rigid, stifling boarding school.

Instead of the algebra and chemistry that fascinated her, chapel started the day, chapel ended the day, and hours of religion and deportment sat in the middle. She resorted to fainting to escape chapel, just as she had done to get out of church in Wendover. But fainting would not bring back Miss Edwards and the nurturing neighborhood

This portrait of Cecilia Payne-Gaposchkin was unveiled in the Faculty Room in University Hall at Harvard University on February 11, 2006. The second woman's picture in the faculty room, Payne-Gaposchkin's portrait was a gift from Professor Dudley R. Herschbach and Georgene B. Herschbach. In the painting, Gaposchkin stands beside one of the wood frames in which astronomers mounted the glass-plate spectrograms they studied as they calculated wavelengths and classified stars.

When Payne-Gaposchkin died in 1979, Charles Whitney of the astronomy staff called her "one of the greatest astronomers in history, and the greatest woman astronomer in history."

school where Cecilia had spent her first six school years.

Cecilia always knew that she wanted to be a scientist and that she would need a university degree to achieve her goal. But universities required courses in math, languages, and science. How could she meet those requirements in this school where her classmates were struggling with long division instead of the quadratic equations she had already mastered? And languages! Instead of the German that universities required, this school taught

French, because ladies should know French. And ladies certainly didn't need science.

The oldest of three children born into an upper-class British family, Cecilia Payne had a quick mind and a passion for understanding the world around her. Wealth and a love of learning did not give her a right to an education, however. Her father died when she was four years old, leaving the family finances strained. Her mother had to make hard choices. When it came to school, Cecilia's younger brother had first call on any money available. Cecilia learned early on that if she was to get an education, it would be up to her.

When she was six years old, she raced to the small, recently opened school just across the street. The teacher promised to teach her to read. Cecilia asked, "Shall I be able to read the *Encyclopedia Britannica?*" To her delight, the teacher assured her that she would learn to read anything she chose. The little girl flung herself into her studies.

When her mother moved the family into London so her brother could attend the right schools for a boy of his social standing, Cecilia was miserable among the many girls with no interest in college. Even her academic successes turned out wrong. When she won a speech competition, for which the prize was a book of her choice, her teachers assumed she would pick a volume of poetry, or maybe Shakespeare. Instead, she horrified them all by asking for a book on fungi. Over and over, Cecilia begged for science and advanced math classes. Finally, the school announced it could do no more for her and asked her to leave.

"It seemed like the end of the world," she wrote in her memoir. "My one desire was to go to Cambridge, and to do so I must win a full scholarship. And now the school had washed its hands of me."

Instead of the end of the world, her dismissal became the perfect beginning. Cecilia wrote that her transfer to St. Paul's Girls' School seemed like a step from medieval to modern times. Outstanding science teachers and well-equipped laboratories contrasted with the idea that ladies couldn't be scientists. "I remember saying to myself: 'I shall never be lonely again; now I can think about science,'" she wrote.

To her delight, Cecilia found much more than just math and science at St. Paul's. The school's music master was the noted musician Gustav Holst. He brought her into the orchestra to play violin, taught her how to conduct, and encouraged her to become a musician. But she loved science more than music and gulped up great gobs of math, physics, and chemistry.

Cecilia won a scholarship to Cambridge when she was seventeen and began to study physics at a revolutionary time in that field. "Radiation was in the air," she said. It had just been discovered. All the great names in physics passed through Cambridge. Some, such as Earnest Rutherford, were on the staff. Others, including Max Plank, were visiting lecturers.

Physics might have been in a state of revolution, but Cambridge was still stuck firmly in the social attitudes of the sixteenth century. Female students were rigidly segregated from male students in lecture halls, in the library, and in laboratories. At least by Cecilia's time, they were allowed to attend classes without a chaperone. One professor objected to having women in his physics laboratory, claiming that their corsets disturbed his magnetic equipment. "Go, take off your corsets!" he would shout at them.

As the only woman in her physics class, Cecilia stood out.

**Margaret Mayall** worked with Annie Cannon at Harvard. Margaret's interest was variable stars and she served as director of AAVSO, the American Association of Variable Star Observers, from 1949 until 1973.

## Stellar Composition

A stellar spectrogram may look a lot like a bar code, but for the women computers at Harvard, identifying the contents of a star was more complicated than scanning for the price of a candy bar. First, the computers had to calculate the wavelength of each dark line. Then, they had to compare the wavelength to known wavelengths of the elements.

The temperatures in stars like our Sun cause their spectra to be misleading. The Sun's spectrum contains mostly iron spectral lines. But Cecilia Payne-Gaposchkin suspected that the Sun consisted largely of hydrogen. In a brilliant insight, she used the emerging science of quantum mechanics to figure this out.

Astronomers still study stars by spectroscopy. But they now use electronic computers to record spectra, calculate wavelengths, and analyze results.

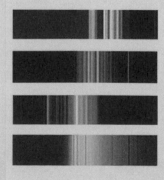

*A group of stellar spectra. These spectra were recorded on photographic film, not the heavy, fragile glass plates the women computers studied for the first decades of stellar spectroscopy.*

Professor Rutherford, who taught the class, began each lecture with a deep "Lady and Gentlemen," while staring fiercely at her, all alone in the front row reserved for women. The boys in the class stamped their feet and shouted to embarrass her. The rudeness of the professor and students was so upsetting it stayed with her all her life. "I still take my place as far back as possible in any lecture room," she said in her autobiography.

Still, Cecilia blossomed at Cambridge. A sociable person, she loved to throw birthday parties for friends, packing as many people as possible into her room. She acted in dramas, played the violin, and conducted both the orchestra and her hall chorus. She loved puns and word play and memorized long nonsense poems.

Then, one evening, she attended a public night at the college observatory and had her first chance to look through a telescope. That one look brought back the night when she and her mother had watched a meteorite paint a flaming arc across the sky. Five-year-old Cecilia had declared on the spot that she would be an astronomer. The visit to the observatory, all those years later,

## Blink Microscope or Comparator

Stars are so far away they appear to stand still, just as a jet plane seems to crawl across the sky. You know the plane is flying at hundreds of miles an hour, but it is more than six miles away. Stars are huge and moving rapidly, but they are light years away. Their movement is even harder to detect.

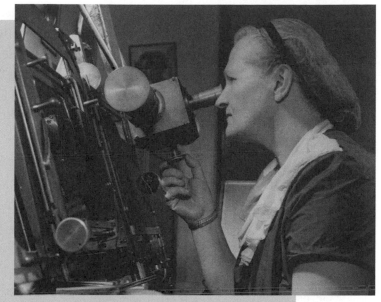

*Cecilia Payne-Gaposchkin at the blink microscope.*

The appearance of creeping is so pronounced we can't detect the motion of even the closest star a mere four light years, or 23,600,000,000,000 miles, away. Planets are closer, so they appear to move much faster than stars. And comets seem to move the fastest of all. But, even these objects are so faraway their motion isn't obvious without long observation.

So, how does an astronomer figure out which point of light is a comet, which a planet, and which a star? The women at Harvard used a blink microscope, also called a blink comparator, the instrument Cecilia Payne-Gaposchkin is using in this photo. The instrument projects two photographs of the same area of the sky directly on top of each other, while the astronomer views the combined image through a magnifying eyepiece. The instrument interrupts the light from first one image, then the other. A change in either the position or the brightness of the object causes the image to jump or flicker while the background remains steady. Knowing the time between the photos allows the astronomer to calculate the movement of the star, or the period of its change in brightness (see also page 142).

"opened the heavens to me," she said.

Eager to show others the wonders of the night sky, Cecilia volunteered to organize and run the public nights at the observatory. She began a journal in which she kept a list of the research questions that interested her. Then she took on a research problem and had the joy of seeing her first paper printed by the Royal Astronomical Society.

In 1922, as she was preparing to graduate from Cambridge, a friend told her that Harlow Shapley had scheduled a public lecture in London. Shapley had just been appointed director of the Harvard College Observatory in America and was touring Europe, visiting other observatories.

Cecilia knew that women had a slightly better chance to work as astronomers in the United States than they had in England. She marched into the lecture determined to meet Director Shapley. When she told him she wanted to work with him, he said, "When Miss Cannon retires, you can succeed her." Cecilia set out for the U. S. within the month, not realizing that Annie Cannon had no intention of retiring and that Shapley had been joking.

Cecilia Payne entered Radcliffe College, the women's college associated with Harvard University, in 1923, as a graduate student in astronomy. Harvard did not admit women students.

Shapley assigned Payne to the problem of determining the chemical composition of the stars and finding out the relative amounts of each chemical element present in each star. She used the stellar spectra that the women at Harvard had been cataloging for more than twenty years. Under the supervision of Annie Cannon, and using the process designed by Antonia Maury, Cecilia analyzed each spectrogram to find out how much iron,

***Antoinette de Vaucouleurs*** was born in Paris, but worked in stellar spectroscopy all over the world. She worked at the London Null Hill Observatory when Margaret Burbidge was acting director. She spent time at the Harvard Observatory in Cambridge, Massachusetts. And she was part of the astronomy department of the University of Texas from 1961 until her death in 1986.

## 1930

Sawyer receives her doctorate, marries Frank Hogg, and moves to Victoria, British Columbia.

magnesium, hydrogen, and other elements each star contained.

Shortly after she began her project, Shapley told Payne that another graduate student, Donald Menzel, would work on the same project. They would not work as partners. Instead, they would be competitors. The director believed that competition between students was good for them, making them tough. Payne said she innocently "subscribed to his idea that one does one's best work when one is miserable."

Payne's research soon revealed that stars were made almost entirely of hydrogen, the lightest element in the universe. The discovery surprised Payne, and she knew that other astronomers would not accept it. They believed stars were huge, and would not believe it possible that they could be composed mostly of light hydrogen atoms instead of heavy metal atoms.

As a graduate student and a woman, Payne did not believe she could argue the point. To insure that her thesis would be accepted by her degree committee, she contradicted her own data and wrote that her values for hydrogen were "improbably high and almost certainly not real." She was not vindicated until other astronomers duplicated her research with the same results. Now we know that stars are almost entirely hydrogen and that their light is produced by fusion of hydrogen atoms into larger atoms. But Payne did receive Harvard's first-ever astronomy PhD in 1925.

**Hazel Marie Losh** received her degrees at the University of Michigan, and held a research faculty position there starting in 1927.

In 1933, with her degree work and her first controversy behind her, Payne traveled to Europe to visit several northern observatories. The political atmosphere was tense in Europe with the conflicts that would eventually lead to World War II. She was horrified by the grim conditions in Russia, where food and clothing were scarce and a feeling of oppression was everywhere. She was glad to head back to Germany for a final meeting.

At the conference in Germany, she met a young Russian astronomer and political refugee named Sergei Gaposchkin, who

## 1934

Payne marries Sergei Gaposchkin. Cecilia Payne-Gaposchkin accepts an academic position at Harvard.

was trying to escape both Russian and German persecution. He introduced himself to Payne and asked her to take his resume back to Harvard with her. He said later that he had expected to meet an old lady and was surprised to find someone his own age.

She was moved by Gaposchkin's plight, and returned to Harvard determined to find a place for him on the Harvard staff. She traveled to Washington, D.C., to arrange for his travel visa.

Mutual respect and admiration between Sergei and Cecilia grew into love. In 1934, she and Sergei married. She took Sergei's name, but in hyphenated form, signing herself Cecilia Payne-Gaposchkin.

Sergei and Cecilia had three children, who grew up in a warm, affectionate household. Her daughter Katherine, writing in the forward to her mother's memoir, described Cecilia as a world traveler, inspired cook, marvelous seamstress, inventive knitter, and voracious reader. The family shared Cecilia's love of music and drama and often produced their own plays and musicals.

Katherine says her mother was tall and dignified, with a regal appearance. Cecilia was nearly six feet tall at a time when the average American woman was about five feet tall. Her height and stature probably intimidated some people. However, some believe her ability to look male astronomers in the eye made her harder to dismiss.

Payne-Gaposchkin's life at Harvard was typical for women in the sciences at that time. She taught astronomy classes, supervised graduate students, and served as acting chair of the astronomy department. Yet she had no official title. For years she was paid a pittance, and her salary came from the director's office-supply budget. Even though she was an officer on the council that directed the Harvard College Observatory, she was forbidden to use the telescope herself unless Sergei was present. She had all the responsibilities but none of the status or salary of the male faculty. Her first a real academic appointment came in 1938, in spite of

National Academy of Sciences elects Payne-Gaposchkin to membership. Helen and Frank Hogg move to Ontario.

her prestigious election to the National Academy of Sciences.

In her autobiography, she described a typical encounter with the director. When a new observatory director was needed, "Harlow Shapley said, 'What this observatory needs is a spectroscopist.' I replied indignantly that I was a spectroscopist. I protested, to no avail; a spectroscopist must be imported."

Finally the graduate student she had originally been forced to compete with became director of the observatory. Donald Menzel told her later that he was shocked

In 1929, the Observatory staff performed the Gilbert and Sullivan musical *HMS Pinafore*, which they re-named *Observatory Pinafore*. Cecilia Payne is second from the left; Helen Sawyer is fifth from the left. Their lyrics included:

> We work from morn till night.
> Computing is our duty.
> We're faithful and polite.
> And our record book's a beauty.

Hogg becomes a research assistant at University of Toronto.

when he saw how low her salary was. He promptly increased her salary to an adequate level.

Cecilia became a full professor of astronomy in 1956, the first woman to be named to such a position at Harvard. She invited all the woman students in astronomy to a party to help her celebrate the event. Her remarks at the party illustrate her undying love of the pun as well as her understanding of the difficulties women faced. "I find myself cast in the unlikely role of the thin wedge," she said, making a double joke about her size and her effort to open science to more women.

One indication of the quality of work done by a scientist is the number of times that person's work is cited in papers by other scientists. The number of citings of Payne-Gaposchkin's work has been among the highest of any astronomer, and has not dropped off following her death.

A life-long heavy smoker, Cecilia Payne-Gaposchkin died of lung cancer in 1979, at the age of 79. Though repeatedly disappointed in her own professional life, Cecilia Payne-Gaposchkin encouraged young women to enter the sciences. To young women Cecilia said, "The reward of the young scientist is the emotional thrill of being the first person in the history of the world to see something or to understand something. Nothing can compare with that experience. The reward of the old scientist is the sense of having seen a vague sketch grow into a masterly landscape." ◉

Some women make their mark in astronomy by discovering a new object or phenomenon in the heavens. Others are best known for sharing their love of star gazing with others. No one was better at encouraging others to revel in the glories of the night sky than Canada's Helen Sawyer Hogg.

*The stars belong to everyone.*

Helen Sawyer Hogg

# HELEN SAWYER HOGG

**born 1905**

**died 1993**

Helen Sawyer clung to her daddy's ears as she sat on his shoulders, shivering in the frosty air. "Sit still and look up, sleepyhead," he said. Five-year-old Helen could hardly believe her eyes. There was a streak of bright light across the sky. "What is it Daddy?" she whispered. "Why that's Halley's Comet," her father told her. "You are one lucky little girl. Many people never see this comet. It only visits the earth every seventy-six years. Isn't it beautiful?"

Fourteen years later, a very cold Helen Sawyer

*Stages of a total
solar eclipse.*

shivered again, this time on an icy Connecticut hillside, watching
a solar eclipse. At nineteen, Helen was majoring in chemistry at
Mount Holyoke College, but she had joined her astronomy class
for the trip to see the solar eclipse. Helen wrote later that "the glory
of the spectacle seems to have tied me to astronomy for life, despite
my horribly cold feet as we stood almost knee deep in snow." Helen
went back to Mount Holyoke, and with the encouragement of Ann
Young, the astronomy professor, changed her major to astronomy.

Her decision was reinforced when Annie Jump Cannon
visited Mount Holyoke a year later and met with Helen several
times. Cannon recommended Helen to Harlow Shapley, the
director of the Harvard Observatory. In the spring of 1926, Helen
began her studies there. She soon found the idea of an expanding
universe irresistible. For her PhD, Helen Sawyer Hogg studied the
same variable star cycles that Henrietta Leavitt had begun studying
at Harvard. Helen's research reinforced the idea of an expanding
universe.

One of the first people Helen met at Harvard was Frank
Hogg, a young Canadian who would be the second student, after
Cecilia Payne-Gaposchkin, to receive a doctorate in astronomy
through the Harvard Observatory. Helen and Frank married in
1930, and Helen received her doctorate — from Radcliffe.

The Hoggs moved to Victoria, British Columbia, to work
at the Dominion Astrophysical Observatory. Frank had a job,

1938

Cannon becomes Professor of Astronomy at Harvard.

Once, in Washington, D.C., Helen Hogg was interviewed by a reporter who asked her if she had brought her telescope with her. *My telescope*, she thought, *is a little job weighing forty tons, with a revolving shelter weighing eighty tons!* The photo shows Hogg with the telescope at the David Dunlap Observatory in Toronto.

## 1939

Peachey graduates from University College in London and marries Geoff Burbidge.

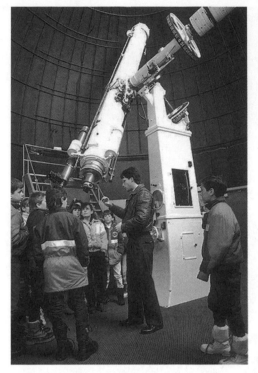

*The 15-inch refracting telescope used by Helen Hogg at the Dominion Observatory has been moved to the Canada Science and Technology Museum in Ottawa and placed in the Helen Sawyer Hogg Observatory.*

but since the observatory would not hire two people from the same family, Helen worked as a volunteer.

In 1929, Edwin Hubble had proposed the Big Bang Theory to explain the expansion of the universe. Hubble theorized that the universe originated in a cosmic explosion from a single very hot point, and that it has been expanding from that explosion ever since. Hubble's theory suggested new lines of research to Helen. She started her own observing program on variable stars in globular clusters. (A globular cluster is a collection of tens of thousands of stars forming a sphere that gathers around a galaxy.)

The Hoggs made a good team. At that time, women were forbidden to spend nights in the dome alone with male technicians. However, since Frank worked in the dome at night, Helen was free to do her observing as well. When their first child, Sally, was tiny, she accompanied her parents to the observatory and spent her nights bundled up in a basket beneath the desk. "Babies sleep most of the time, anyway," said Helen.

In 1935, the family moved to Ontario, and Helen continued her research program at the David Dunlap Observatory. A year later, she was appointed to the position of research assistant at the University of Toronto, which operates the Dunlap Observatory. And it was in Ontario that Sally's two brothers, David and James, were born.

Fortunately, Helen's early experiences in astronomy prepared her for the difficulties of observational astronomy. Working in an observatory at night in Northern Canada is a challenge.

1941

Annie Cannon dies.  Beatrice Hill is born in Chester, England.

Telescopes must be kept at the same temperatures as the surrounding atmosphere—even when that temperature is extremely cold. Warming causes moisture to condense on the mirrors and destroys the focus. Heat also creates differences in air density, which produces currents of air. The currents make objects appear to shimmer. To get good results, observatories are not heated. Some Canadian astronomers wear heated flight suits during the winter.

Helen Hogg was a busy, active researcher, as well as a busy, active mother. She traveled to Sweden to attend the International Astronomical Union General Assembly. She spent time at the Steward Observatory in Arizona, photographing globular clusters that were too far south to be seen from the Dunlap Observatory. She took three hundred research plates in six weeks at Steward. In 1940, she was appointed Acting Chair of the Astronomy Department at Mount Holyoke. In 1941, she took on a teaching assignment at the University of Toronto replacing one of the men who had joined the army.

During World War II (1941-1946), most able-bodied young men in Canada and America served in the military overseas. Frank Hogg, who had a heart ailment, remained at the Dunlap Observatory along with another man and two women, Helen Hogg and Ruth Northcott. The four ran the observatory at nights and taught classes by day. "Hard years," Helen called them. Five years after the war, Frank Hogg died suddenly of a heart attack in 1951.

For thirty years, Helen Hogg wrote a weekly article on astronomy for *The Toronto Star*, making her name known to

***Paris Pismis,*** a Turkish astronomer who worked as an assistant astronomer for a year at Harvard in 1938, married mathematician Felix Recillas and settled in Mexico. She helped establish Mexico's importance in astronomical education and research.

***Janet Hanula Akyuz Mattei,*** also Turkish, earned her PhD in 1982 from Ege University in Turkey with research on dwarf novae.

1943
Jocelyn Bell is born in Ireland.

1944
Jill Tarter is born in New York.

1947
Margaret Geller is born in Ithaca, New York.

Helen Hogg in a photo taken at the IAU Conference on Globular Systems in Galaxies in Cambridge, Massachusetts, August 1986.

Globular Cluster M80 is a very dense cluster containing several hundred thousand stars. The high density creates large gravitational attractions which hold the cluster together. The cluster is about 28,000 light years away from Earth, in the direction of the constellation Scorpius.

millions of Canadians. The title of the popular book on astronomy she wrote, *The Stars Belong to Everyone*, reflects her life-long passion to introduce readers to the joy of star watching.

Hogg published three editions of *Catalogues of Variable Stars in Globular Clusters*, the last in 1973. Her catalogs are valuable references and are frequently cited by other astronomers. She was working on a fourth edition at the time of her death in 1993.

Helen Hogg was an international expert on variable stars in globular clusters. She discovered hundreds of new variable stars and published more than two hundred papers. People called her knowledge of the night sky phenomenal. Even on cloudy nights when she was scheduled to observe, she always watched for breaks in the clouds just in case one of "her clusters" might appear. ◉

# More Questions Than Answers

Even with the best telescopes, astronomers can't see through fog and clouds or ignore the distorting effect of the miles of earthly atmosphere between the lens and distant stars. After decades of struggling to find good equipment and clear skies, Margaret Burbidge led the team that designed the Hubble Space Telescope and let all astronomers triumph over the problems of earth-bound observations.

*Seeing that image produced such euphoria that I felt it was almost sinful to be enjoying astronomy so much.*

Margaret Burbidge

# MARGARET PEACHEY BURBIDGE

**born 1919**

The wail of the air-raid siren cut through the foggy night. Margaret Peachey quickly tucked away the spectrogram she had been studying, grabbed her coat and scarf, and hurried to join the rest of the observatory staff in the bomb shelter. Every night for a week, they had spent long hours in the subways as German bombs rained down on London.

Each time an explosion shook the lights and sprinkled those sitting on platform and tracks with concrete dust, twenty-year-old Margaret

*The people of London used subway tunnels as bomb shelters during the war. In this photo the rails are cemented over. Nearly two hundred thousand people slept in the tunnels every night. Volunteer civil defense proctors handed out food, drink, and first-aid supplies.*

worried about how much damage the flying shrapnel might do to the equipment and buildings of University College London's observatory. She wondered how much repair work she would have to arrange for the next day. She hoped the old and slightly crotchety telescope would not be completely destroyed. Finding functioning equipment and hours of clear sky in which to do her research was always a struggle. Perhaps, when the all-clear sounded, she needed to start looking for somewhere else to pursue her PhD.

Margaret Peachey's love of science was a family trait. Her mother studied chemistry at Manchester School of Technology, and had planned to become a chemist. Instead, she married her handsome chemistry teacher. Also an inventor, Margaret's father had patented an important process for the vulcanization of rubber. The Peacheys moved to London so he could market his process. Margaret was born there in 1919. Her sister arrived three years later, in 1922.

Margaret's parents encouraged their daughters to read, study, and explore the world around them. To share their love of the natural world, the Peacheys gave their children books on flowers, plants, and trees. "My sister and I became passionate tree climbers," Margaret wrote in her memoir. Further feeding their daughters' curiosity, the family subscribed to a children's newspaper. One monthly feature illustrated the phases of the moon and ignited Margaret's life-long interest in lunar phases. A chemistry set and a microscope rounded out her tools for exploring the world.

1948

Vera Cooper graduates from Vassar and marries Robert Rubin.

Margaret fell in love with numbers before she started school. In her memoir, she describes becoming enchanted with very large numbers, those with lots of zeros, which she could "write out and think about." Eight years later, when her grandfather gave her a set of popular astronomy books, she learned that astronomers dealt with such numbers routinely. Alpha Centauri A, the nearest star to us, is 26,000,000,000,000 miles away. Fascinated by such lovely numbers, she decided that when she grew up, she wanted to be the one who measured the distances to the stars.

When she enrolled in University College London in 1936, she took physics, math, and chemistry, thinking she might study chemistry, like her mother. When she found that UCL offered a major in astronomy with a minor in math, her career path was set. She continued to take every physics and chemistry course she could, laying a firm foundation for her future research.

Graduation is normally a festive time, but when Margaret graduated from UCL in 1939, Britain was preparing for war with Germany. The war that began on September 1 of that year defined the new graduate's early years as an astronomer. Small children filled trains out of London

## The Impact of World War II on Astronomy

World War II upended the lives of Europeans and North Americans alike. Astronomers Margaret Burbidge and Helen Hogg put their careers on hold when they stepped into vacancies left by men who were drafted.

Many German astronomers and physicists made harrowing journeys to escape the German secret police, called the Gestapo. Russian cosmologists George Gamov and Sergei Gaposchkin took advantage of the chaos of the war to flee from an oppressive government and make their way to American universities. And sadly, many promising young scientists died in the war. More than three million young men died between 1939 and 1945, robbing the world of almost a full generation of future astronomers.

Following the war, Congress enacted the GI Bill, which provided American veterans with college tuition. A few aspiring astronomers completed their educations under the Bill. But since few women were in the military, and universities were closing their graduate programs to women, the number of women astronomers declined rapidly for the next thirty years.

1949

Roman receives her doctorate from University of Chicago. Spellman graduates from University of California at Chico.

on their way to the relative safety of the countryside. Rationed food and fuel became more and more scarce. Night after night, Nazi bombs pounded English cities.

The people of Britain threw themselves into the war effort. Most men joined the military, and civilians volunteered for jobs either in civil defense, or as replacements for the missing men. Although just graduated from the university, Margaret was responsible for running the observatory. She managed the buildings, supervised the maintenance of equipment, and arranged repairs to buildings damaged in the bombing.

Early in the war, Margaret supervised military projects for the Ministry of Defense. In one, she directed assembly of an instrument that measures the approach, angle, and speed of an attacking aircraft. Another project she directed allowed military strategists to assess the results of allied bombs on enemy targets.

After the war, Margaret looked for a place to do her graduate research. She loved working in an open dome under the stars. But the equipment she used was out of date, and the constant fog and rain of London made viewing impossible

*Margaret Peachey, center, with friends during the war. Rationing of materials and gasoline made private cars a rarity and motor bikes popular.*

more nights than not. "My aim," she said, was "access to larger telescopes, better instruments, and clear skies."

To gain that access, she applied for a Carnegie Fellowship at the Mt. Wilson Observatory in Pasadena, California. There she ran into her first experience of blatant discrimination. "The turn-down letter simply pointed out that Carnegie Fellowships were available only for men," she wrote. Reluctantly, Margaret continued her graduate studies at UCL. But the quest for viewing time on the world's best telescopes became a major

1951                                                    1952

Spellman marries Gene Shoemaker. Sally Ride is born in Encino, California. Frank Hogg dies.          Antonia Maury dies.

theme of her professional career.

In 1947, she took a course on atomic spectra where she met fellow student Geoffrey Burbidge, whom she married in 1948. After their graduations, the couple began their professional life. They pieced together research grants, fellowships, summer conferences, and post-doctoral appointments all over the U.S. and Europe. Their appointments were often at different institutions, and they lived apart frequently, a very early "commuter marriage."

For several years they wandered from coast to coast across the United States and bounced back and forth across the Atlantic Ocean. Finally, they found themselves in Cambridge, England, where they began a research collaboration with astronomers Willy Fowler and Fred Hoyle.

Margaret had been studying Cecilia Payne-Gaposchkin's research on the abundance of hydrogen in stars. She and Geoff became increasingly interested in the way heavier elements might form in stars. Along with Fowler and Hoyle, they began to work out a theory to explain the way elements such as iron are produced from hydrogen in stars.

As their time at Cambridge came to a close, the Burbidges again applied for fellowships in the U.S. This time, knowing the ban on selecting women for Carnegie Fellowships, Fowler arranged a fellowship for Margaret at the Kellogg Radiation Laboratory at California Institute of Technology in Pasadena. Geoff obtained the Carnegie Fellowship. Finally, they both had grants that would pay the bills, and the institutions were close together in California.

Geoff's fellowship granted him telescope time at Mt. Wilson. It included lodging, meals, and transportation to and from the observatory. Margaret needed to use the large telescope for her research, but since she was not the one with the grant, nor the meals and lodging, the couple worked out a complicated agreement.

*The Mt. Wilson Observatory sits in the San Gabriel Mountains near Pasadena, California, on 5715-foot Mt. Wilson. George Hale founded it in 1904 and became its first director. The air around Mt. Wilson is particularly calm, aiding observations.*

## 1957

Margaret would use some of Geoff's viewing time unofficially. They would stay in a small, unheated summer cottage near the telescope, provide their own transportation, and bring their own lunches. At first, they even ate by themselves, away from the rest of the observatory staff. Before long, however, the on-site technicians at Mt. Wilson told them that eating separately was nonsense, and Geoff and Margaret joined the communal meal in the observatory galley.

The Burbidges' creativity in working around roadblocks paid off. In 1957, along with Fowler and Hoyle, they published a long paper outlining the processes by which heavier elements could be made out of hydrogen in the nuclear furnace of a star. The paper, now a classic, is referred to in shorthand as B2FH, for the names of the researchers. It established their reputations. It also earned a Nobel Prize for Fowler, but not for Hoyle or either of the Burbidges.

The Burbidges were, however, offered positions at the University of Chicago's Yerkes Observatory. As successful astronomers and new parents of a baby girl, they were finally able to establish a real home.

At that time, the University of Chicago had a rule against two members of a family being on the same faculty. Geoff got the faculty position, and Margaret got a fellowship, a position of lower salary and lower prestige. For the next five years, they observed at Yerkes on the 82-inch McDonald telescope.

As an observational astronomer, Margaret has learned the hard way that astronomy can be physically dangerous. Astronomers work in the dark, around moving equipment. One night, she accidently stepped over the edge of the viewing platform and fell about ten feet down to the main deck. Then, a motor moving equipment around the telescope rim jammed and trapped Geoff's arm, nearly breaking it. Fortunately, they both survived with just small cuts and bruises.

George Hale built the original 40-inch telescope at Yerkes Observatory in 1897. Located in Williams Bay, Wisconsin, the observatory is a facility of the Department of Astronomy and Astrophysics of the University of Chicago.

1957

timeline continued on page 122

Burbidges publish B2FH to acclaim. Wendy Freedman is born in Toronto.

# Optical Telescopes

Galileo demonstrated in 1609 the wonders that could be seen through a telescope. He set off a frenzy of new telescope design and improvement. Galileo's scope was a refracting telescope. Refraction occurs when a light ray is bent as it passes from one material to another. Refraction allows an image to be magnified as light passes through a set of transparent lenses.

Astronomers soon found that bigger lenses with greater distances between them made the image larger. In 1722, James Bradley made a telescope with a focal length of 212 feet. Long telescopes like this were not made in tubes. Instead, scientists mounted lenses on a long pole in the open air. Astronomers called these long telescopes air scopes.

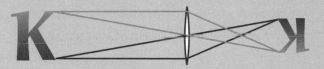

Isaac Newton discovered a flaw in refracting telescopes that caused fuzzy images. Different wavelengths of light are bent different degrees when they pass through a lens. Although very slight, the differences are enough to distort the images. To fix the problem, Newton decided to build a reflecting telescope. With this instrument, the image is magnified with curved mirrors rather than transparent lenses. In 1671, Newton designed and built the world's first reflecting telescope using a highly polished metal surface. His telescope magnified objects thirty-eight times with little distortion.

These days, astronomers use both reflecting and refracting telescopes. Special techniques have been developed to allow the use of refractors that do not distort images.

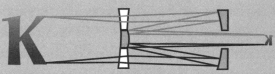

*Margaret Burbidge selects slides and images for a talk at the American Astronomical Society.*

In 1963, the Burbidges moved to the University of California to begin a study of quasars. As their reputations rose, the couple also began to speak out on the problem of discrimination against women in astronomy. When the American Astronomical Society told Margaret that they were giving her the Annie Jump Cannon Prize, available only to women, she decided she was well enough known to do something for women. She wrote a letter declining the prize, saying, "It is high time that discrimination in favor of, as well as against women in professional life, be removed." The letter ignited controversy but got the issue before the association. Among the responses to her letter, she said, was a note from Beatrice Tinsley, "expressing her strong approval of my action."

Continuing her efforts to end discrimination against women, Margaret encouraged the American Astronomical Society to hold conferences only in states that had ratified the proposed Equal Rights Amendment to the U.S. Constitution (see page 64).

Late in 1971, Margaret became director of the Royal Greenwich Observatory in England, where she found gender discrimination alive and well. Unlike her male predecessors for the previous 300 years, she was not also named Astronomer Royal.

As the observatory director, she was back in the struggle for adequate telescopes and good seeing. The staff seethed with controversy, split between those who wanted to move the observatory to a better site and those who wanted to keep it where it had been for hundreds of years. The best sites in the world manage two thousand observing hours a year. The Greenwich telescope averaged six hundred to eight hundred hours. The telescope was eventually moved to La Palma, in the Canary Islands. Margaret was fed up with tension and strife, and she resigned after less than two years at Greenwich.

Astronomers all over the world shared Margaret's dream of better

## The Sloan Digital Sky Survey

Think about this comparison: In the forty years she spent classifying stars by their spectra, Annie Cannon produced a catalog of more than 300,000 stars. In its first five years of operation, the Sloan Digital Sky Survey (SDSS) looked at nearly five hundred million galaxies and more than 500,000 specific stars, recording data on the position, brightness, and color of each.

Operating from the Apache Point Observatory in New Mexico, the SDSS uses detectors called charge-coupled devices, or CCDs. They are 100 times more sensitive than photographic plates, and they produce digital data at a rate of nearly 640 spectra at a time.

*Constance Rockosi, a graduate student at the University of Chicago and member of the team that built the scanning camera for the SDSS, checks the instrument during its trial runs in 1988.*

Data flows so rapidly into the SDSS that astronomer Gillian Knapp, writing in the August 1997 issue of the magazine *Sky and Telescope,* compared the flood to drinking from a fire hose. The CCD chips fill up enough

Gillian Knapp

CDs in a single night to play for more than 250 hours. The data is recorded in computer databases so astronomers can locate information rapidly. The data "will do us no good if we can't analyze them during a human lifetime," said Knapp.

A joint effort of government, university, and independent observatories all over the world, the SDSS lets astronomers locate new galaxies, analyze redshifts, and add to our knowledge of the structure of the universe. As Knapp says, the biggest payoff in any new, unprecedented view of the heavens is likely to be in the surprises it provides.

*King Charles II established the Greenwich Royal Observatory in 1675 and gave the head astronomer the title of Astronomer Royal. The observatory is also the site of the Prime Meridian, the basis of longitude measurement, and the source of Greenwich Mean Time, or Universal Time. The astronomy functions now operate in the Canary Islands, and the base for Universal Time may soon lose out to atomic clocks.*

telescopes, better instruments, and clear skies. In the 1970s, NASA and the European Space Agency began to design an orbiting space telescope. Given the dismal viewing conditions Margaret had experienced, first at the UCL Observatory, then at Greenwich, her participation in the development of the Hubble Space Telescope may seem like the most exciting part of her career. Finally, astronomers would have a telescope far above the UV-absorbing ozone layer of the Earth, one not vulnerable to fog, clouds, city lights, and the distorting effects of Earth's atmosphere.

After serving on the Space Science Board and helping to develop the concept of a space telescope, Margaret was appointed to head the design team when the University of California at San Diego won the contract. After many delays and cost overruns by manufacturers, the Hubble Space Telescope launched in 1990.

Young Margaret Peachey's dream was not yet a reality, however. Errors in grinding the enormous mirror of the telescope caused a distortion that made images through the Hubble only slightly better than those from telescopes still bound to Earth. Astronauts on a servicing mission in 1993 installed instruments that corrected the distortion. Finally the Hubble lived up to its expectations.

Of her first view of images from the repaired Hubble, Margaret wrote that it produced a euphoria. She was seeing light from a distant galaxy never before seen by human eyes. After a lifetime of effort, Margaret Peachey Burbidge had helped free astronomers of the problems of Earth-bound astronomy. She gave the world an eye to the heavens that reaches millions of light years out into the universe. ◉

Fog, clouds, and light pollution limit the effectiveness of even the biggest optical telescopes on Earth. Astronomers who study ultraviolet or X-ray emission of stars have been more limited because Earth's atmosphere blocks almost all of that radiation. Nancy Roman has devoted her career to designing telescopes that orbit the Earth. Outside the Earth's atmosphere, these telescopes easily detect and measure gamma ray, X-ray, and ultraviolet wavelengths.

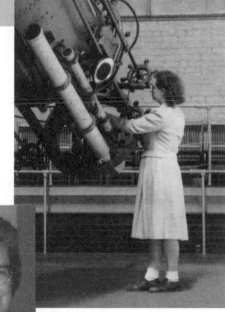

*Mother of the Hubble Space Telescope*

Swarthmore College Newsletter

# NANCY GRACE ROMAN

**born 1925**

Whispers and giggles floated up through the dark as the girls of the sixth-grade Astronomy Club spread their blankets on the lawn of the Roman family's backyard.

"I see Orion."

"Look! There's Cassiopeia."

"Do you think we'll see any meteorites tonight?"

This would be the last star party for the club. When school started next week, twelve-year-old Nancy Roman and her friends would be going to bed too early for star watching. After tonight, they would meet inside and study star charts to learn the names of stars and constellations.

Born in Nashville, Tennessee, Nancy Roman says she can't recall a time when she was not determined to be an astronomer and to learn everything she could about stars. Her father, Irwin, was a U.S. Geological Survey geophysicist who encouraged her interest in science. Many of her friends and teachers tried to discourage Nancy from studying astronomy, telling her it was not a field for women. But she persisted, and read every astronomy book she could find in school and city libraries. "I am glad I was stubborn," she says now. "I have had a wonderful career."

After high school, Nancy studied astronomy at Swarthmore College in Pennsylvania, where she worked at the Sproul Observatory. She studied for her PhD in astronomy at the University of Chicago and worked at the Yerkes Observatory, earning her degree in 1949. Roman did research at the McDonald Observatory in West Texas also. "In those days, we could get substantial telescope time, and I often spent as much as four months a year at [McDonald]," she said in an interview. "I enjoyed both research and teaching, but forty years ago it was nearly impossible for a woman to get tenure in an astronomy research department. Therefore, I left the university to join the radio astronomy branch at the Naval Research Laboratory."

Roman's focus in astronomy has always been to try to understand the nature of stars. In her effort to understand the life cycle of stars, she used optical, radio, and X-ray telescopes. In time, other astronomers also became more interested in the formation and evolution of stars. "Where they used to think it would be possible to identify all the stars in the sky, now they don't try so hard to discover more stars as to understand the ones we know about," says Roman. "The Milky Way holds enough stars for anyone."

At the U.S. Naval Research Observatory, she worked in radio astronomy and was soon named head of the microwave spectroscopy section. Roman loved research. But a chance observation made earlier in West Texas was about to change her career completely.

While collecting data on high velocity stars at McDonald Observatory, she noticed that a star she was studying did not match the published data about it. The information described the star as being very like our own Sun. But Roman saw that it was very different. "It didn't look anything at all like the Sun," she said. She published her observation in a short paper in *The Astrophysical Journal* and thought no more about that star. Others did think about it, however.

Her short paper caught the attention of a Russian astronomer, who invited her to be a speaker at the dedication of a major new Russian observatory. She was one of just three American astronomers invited to the event, and her public trip to Russia generated headlines in U.S. newspapers. The publicity brought Roman to the attention of NASA administrators. "I was asked if I knew anyone who would like to set up a program in space astronomy," she said in an interview. "I knew that taking on that responsibility would mean that I could no longer do forefront research. But the challenge of starting with a clean slate, to formulate a program that would influence astronomy for decades to come, was too great to resist."

For nearly twenty years, Nancy Roman designed the orbiting instruments that detect

## Non-optical Telescopes

By the middle of the twentieth century, astronomers realized that stars emit the full spectrum of electromagnetic radiation. That was both good and bad news. The good news was that high energy emissions, such as X-rays and radio waves, would be detectable on Earth. Designers immediately began work on telescopes that could detect these emissions.

The bad news was that low-energy emissions, such as infrared radiation, would not penetrate the Earth's atmosphere. Detection of the infrared emissions put out by a star would have to be detected by telescopes away from the Earth. Astronomers eagerly developed satellite telescopes and launched the first X-ray telescope in 1970, shown here. It was named Uhuru, which means "freedom" in Swahili, the language of Kenya, where it rocketed into space.

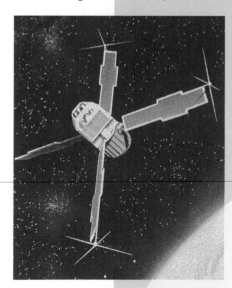

*Nancy Roman, as Chief of the Astronomy Program in NASA's Physics and Astronomy Programs Office, explains the Advanced Orbiting Solar Observatory (AOSO) satellite to astronaut Edwin (Buzz) Aldrin.*

and measure gamma rays, radio waves, X-rays, and visible light. Among Roman's satellite observatories were three solar observatories that use ultraviolet light and X-rays to study the Sun. She was also responsible for the launch of three small astronomical satellites that use X-ray and gamma-rays to study the sky, one International Ultraviolet Explorer, and four astronomical observatories that make optical and ultraviolet measurements.

*Launch of the Delta rocket, which carried the OSO 8 into orbit in June, 1975.*

The programs she directed gave astronomers important information about planet surfaces and led to the successful Viking probes that landed on Mars in 1976. Roman helped design and produce nearly all the orbiting observatories launched during the 1970s and 1980s. She collected data from the ultraviolet and X-ray detecting Copernicus satellite in 1972, and from the U.S. space station Skylab that circled the Earth from 1973 until 1979.

*Skylab orbited Earth from 1973 to 1979; then, it broke into pieces in the atmosphere upon re-entry over Perth, Australia.*

Roman's most important contribution to orbiting telescopes may have been her participation in the design of the Hubble space telescope. Her tireless efforts lobbying NASA and Congress eventually obtained funds to build the world's first orbiting optical telescope.

Using the Hubble Space Telescope, optical astronomy advanced farther in fifteen years than it had in the previous fifty years before the Hubble. The stunning images sent to Earth by the Hubble have increased public interest in astronomy as well as understanding of our universe. Images provided by HST are available to any person at the NASA web site.

Now retired from NASA, Roman serves as a consulting astronomer to NASA and a senior scientist for the Astronomical Data Center at NASA's Goddard Space Flight Center. The ADC collects astronomical data from researchers worldwide, converts it into digital catalogs, and makes the information available to astronomers all over the world.

*Above: Nancy Roman with one of the Orbiting Solar Observatories she designed while at NASA. Below: Roman continues her interest in education, volunteering with the organization Retired Scientists, Engineers & Technicians. Here she works with a student on a science project.*

After twenty-one years of designing and launching orbiting telescopes that gathered data unobtainable on Earth, Nancy Roman now continues the tradition of Harvard women whose enormous amounts of data supported astronomy for the first half of the last century. Instead of pens and paper, Roman uses a computer. Instead of depending on steamships or telegraph to distribute data, Roman sends and receives data over the Internet. Still, like the women at Harvard, she provides much of the glue that holds astronomical research together. ◉

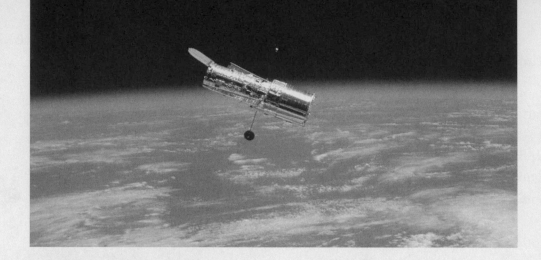

## The Hubble Space Telescope

Astronomer Lyman Spitzer spoke for many in 1964 when he proposed building and launching an orbiting telescope. More than twenty years passed, however, before NASA made firm plans for a large space-based telescope. Struggles for funding continued until 1978, when design and development began, with a launch date set for 1983. Technical problems, cost overruns, delays, and the *Challenger* disaster (see page 149) all slowed development. NASA sent Hubble Space Telescope into orbit on April 24, 1990.

Even after launch, problems remained. A grinding flaw in Hubble's enormous mirror distorted the images so that they were only slightly better than those obtained from the ground. Astronauts on the first servicing mission installed several instruments that corrected the flaw. Nearly fifty years after it had been proposed, the Hubble sent the world's astronomers the first exciting images from space — images that have resulted in recalculation of the size and age of the universe. Data and images from the Hubble Space Telescope are available to the public at http://archive.stsci.edu/hst.

Astronomers publish or present more than five hundred papers a year based on their Hubble observations. However, use of the telescope is not limited to astronomers connected with observatories. Anyone can apply for time on the Hubble Space Telescope, but competition is fierce. Applicants ask for nearly ten times as much time as is available.

In its quest to see farther out into the universe and obtain images of greater detail than even the Hubble can produce, NASA plans to launch a second-generation space telescope in 2014.

Some astronomers' research produced astonishing results—results that challenged old ideas. And some astronomers had trouble accepting new ideas, especially when those ideas came from women. That was the case when Vera Rubin discovered that ninety percent of the universe appeared to be missing.

*We became astronomers thinking we were studying the universe, and now we learn that we are just studying the five or ten percent that is luminous.*

Vera Rubin

# VERA RUBIN

### born 1928

The big box of used books drew twelve-year-old Vera Cooper like a magnet. She happily pawed through the dusty volumes, looking for treasure, and snatched up an astronomy book. What a find! Twenty-five cents would wipe out her allowance, but it would be worth it. She could find answers to her questions by herself. No need to bother an adult.

Back home, she curled up on her bed and flipped to the back of the book. But where was the index? How could she find the topics that interested her without an index? With a sigh, she got out a tablet and a pen, turned to the first chapter, and began to read. Painstakingly, she worked through the entire book, wrote down topics, and noted page numbers. After many long hours, she had her own index. In the process of creating it, she had learned a great deal of astronomy.

Vera's north-facing bedroom window gave her a clear view of the night sky. She often fell asleep watching the slow procession of stars around the North Star. Tracing the trail of each blazing meteor, she began to think of the stars as her own special friends.

Her parents, Philip and Rose, encouraged Vera's interest in astronomy. They introduced her to scientist friends who invited her to use their telescopes. When she was fourteen, her father, an electrical engineer, helped her build her own telescope and took her to meetings of amateur astronomy groups.

Vera's mom passed on her gift for music and her love of reading to her daughter. Reading helped lead Vera to astronomy. When she read a story about Maria Mitchell, she learned that a woman could be an astronomer.

Vera's father supported her interest, but he thought jobs in astronomy were scarce. He encouraged her to major in mathematics instead. He believed that women, in particular, would find more jobs in mathematics than in astronomy.

Her father's concern came true when Swarthmore College, in Pennsylvania, rejected Vera's college application. The Swarthmore admissions officer suggested she find a more ladylike career than astronomy. Perhaps she could paint stars and comets.

Turned down by Swarthmore, Vera received a scholarship to Vassar, where Maria Mitchell had taught. She first considered a career in music composition. But she decided she was not skillful enough to be a professional composer, and turned her hand to astronomy, instead. However, her love of music did help shape her future. "Towards the end of my college years, I met a young man who interested me very much. And among the many things he did that were very nice was that he found a phonograph record of this Hindemith viola sonata [a recording she had been trying to find]. He is now my husband, and this has become a favorite of both of ours."

Vera may have caught a brief glimpse of her professional future on the one-hundredth anniversary of Maria Mitchell's comet discovery, October 1, 1947. The occasion came and went without any mention, even at Vassar. Looking back, Vera said, "Perhaps on that day one of my friends or I irreverently tied a bright scarf around the stern-looking bust of Mitchell in a niche of the observatory building, where she taught for many years. But she deserved more."

Three years after entering Vassar, Vera graduated with a BS in astronomy. Her struggle for acceptance continued when she applied to the graduate astrophysics center at Princeton. Sir Hugh Taylor, dean of the graduate school, wrote back to her that Princeton did not accept women in the graduate physics and astronomy programs. He refused to even send her a catalog. It would be twenty-five more years before Princeton accepted women into graduate programs: physics in 1971, astronomy in 1975, and mathematics in 1976.

Vera decided to go to Cornell, where her new husband, Robert Rubin, was a graduate student in physics. She and Robert had married when she was just twenty years old, right after she finished her degree at Vassar. "I was very conventional," she said in an interview. "I married right as I graduated from college, which was what everyone was doing."

Vera Cooper Rubin completed her master's degree in astronomy only to find that she still couldn't land a job. Even the chairman of the astronomy department told her to find something else to study. "He pointed out there were so few

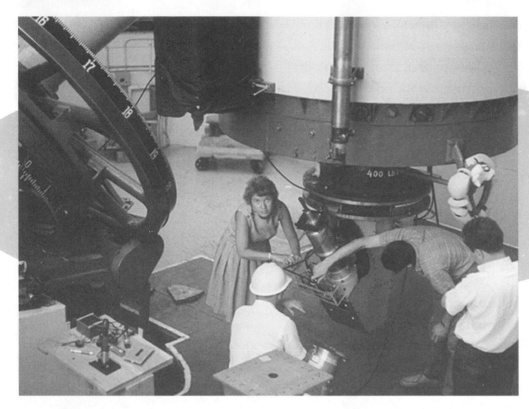

*Astronomers work at the forefront of technology as well as theory. Here Vera Rubin works with engineers and other astronomers, adjusting the equipment she will use for observing.*

observatories, the country didn't need astronomers, and that I couldn't possibly find a job later on."

Besides the usual problems of being a woman astronomer, Rubin's research produced ideas that flew in the face of existing beliefs. One of these was the idea that galaxies rotate around some center in the universe. When Rubin presented her research at the American Astronomical Society meeting in 1950, the audience scoffed at her findings. They said she had too little data to support her conclusions. The conference organizers almost refused to allow her to present her paper. Every top astronomy journal refused to publish it. The media loved her ideas, however, and she made headlines in *The Washington Post* and other newspapers.

After she completed her master's degree, Rubin left astronomy research and settled down to be a wife and mother.

While she raised four children, three boys and a girl, she kept up with astronomy, eagerly reading each month's *Astrophysical Journal*. Before long, she found herself crying over each new issue. The world of astronomy was passing her by.

When she shared her frustrations with Robert, he told her she had to get a PhD. "Don't worry about the details," he told her. "We'll work it out." And they did. For two years, as Vera worked on her doctorate at Georgetown University, Rubin's parents cared for the children. Robert drove her to the university and ate his supper sandwich in the car while she attended her evening classes.

The physics department at Georgetown bristled with excitement. She rubbed shoulders with Nobel Prize winners Hans Bethe and Richard Feynman. George Gamow, a famous early proponent of the Big Bang theory, supervised her research.

*Rubin, like all astronomers, spends far more time analyzing and studying photos and data than she does actually observing.*

As Vera continued to study galaxies, she discovered they were clumped together, not spread evenly throughout the universe. It was as if she had found that the chips in chocolate-chip cookies were in big clumps, when other astronomers believed the chips were all an equal distance from each other. Again, her data was controversial. Mainstream astronomers believed that the Big Bang would have spread galaxies evenly, and they were determined not to be contradicted. Years later, science has again proven Vera Rubin right. Galaxies appear to exist in clumps.

After getting her doctorate, Rubin continued to teach and do research at Georgetown, the only

*Vera Rubin prepares for a night of observation.*

place she could find work. Then, in 1957, Russia launched the first satellite, *Sputnik I,* and interest in astronomy and space exploded. Newspapers and magazines carried stories about astronomy. Science educators redesigned textbooks. America set out to educate and employ more scientists, including astronomers.

Old attitudes were hard to overcome, however. Women were still prohibited from using the larger telescopes, such as the two-hundred-inch telescope on Palomar Mountain in California, and the Inter-American Telescope in Cerro Tololo, Chile. Palomar did not lift the restriction against women until the mid-1960s. Male astronomers continued to call the living quarters at observatories "monasteries."

Rubin was the first woman permitted to schedule time on the telescope at Palomar, in 1965. Vera pinned a female silhouette next to the sign "Men" on the bathroom door. Her cutout always disappeared shortly after she left the observatory.

In 1964, Rubin went to work at the Department of Terrestrial Magnetism, part of the Carnegie Institution in Washington, D.C. At the DTM, she returned to her major interest, the movement of galaxies. Using newly designed instruments, she again found that our galaxy, the Milky Way, and all the galaxies around us, are being drawn toward some distant point. Again astronomers insisted she had to be wrong. Some even wrote to Rubin urging her to give up this line of research. Rubin said her team "interpreted what we observed as a large motion of our own galaxy. I guess that was not easy for some people to believe." Not until the late 1980s did other astronomers verify her findings. They began to refer to the source of the pull on galaxies as the Great Attractor.

Because of the controversy, Rubin redirected her research to the study of the rotation of spiral galaxies around their centers. According to the laws of physics, a galaxy should behave like a solar system. For example, in our solar system, the inner planets orbit the

## The Legacy of *Sputnik I*

If you were an eighth-grader back in 1957 when Russia launched *Sputnik I*, the world's first artificial satellite, you had a front-row seat to the radical change in the way science was taught and conducted in the United States. One year after the launch, President Eisenhower announced the formation of NASA, the National Aeronautical and Space Agency. Ten years later, NASA put the first human — an American — on the surface of the Moon.

In the ten years between *Sputnik I* and *Apollo 11*, scientists and teachers rewrote science courses for high school and colleges, and recruited more science majors, this time including women. NASA's effort to outdo the Russian feat ignited a fascination with space exploration in the American public, and fueled technical advances that continue to drive today's technical economy.

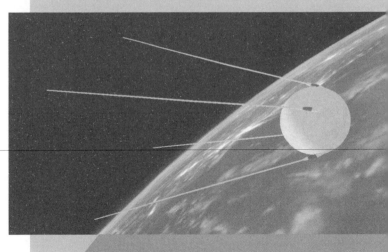

## The Riddle of Dark Matter

Vera Rubin found that the mass of many galaxies was too small to account for the speed with which the outer stars moved. Most of the objects we can see in the night sky are those that shine with their own light, such as stars, or those that reflect light, such as moons. When the mass of the things we could see fell short of the mass required, many astronomers concluded that there was an enormous amount of matter in space that we simply couldn't see, matter they called dark matter.

The calculations that relate mass and the movement of stars in galaxies depends on the force of gravity, a force we thought we understood. But what if we don't really understand gravity? Is it possible that, on the scale of a galaxy, gravity does not behave the way we think it does? Questions like these are producing exciting new theories about the origin and behavior of the universe, and promise to keep astronomers busy for a long time.

Sun much faster than the outer planets. The faster a planet orbits, the greater is its tendency to fly away from the Sun. For each planet, the tendency to fly away is exactly balanced by the gravitational attraction between the Sun and the planet. As a result, the planet stays in its orbit.

The gravitational attraction between the Sun and the planet decreases the farther away the planet is from the Sun. So, the farther away a planet, the slower it moves. If the outer planets orbited as rapidly as the inner ones, the Sun's gravity could not hold them in their orbits. They would fly off into space like drops of water flung away from a rotating water sprinkler.

Astronomers had believed that the total mass of stars in a galaxy produced just enough gravity to balance the energy of each individual star and keep it attached to the galaxy.

Rubin discovered that the outer stars of many galaxies orbit the core so fast they should fly away. The gravity needed to hold galaxies together is far too great to be generated by the mass of the stars we see in them. Rubin's discovery forced astronomers to ask a fundamental new question: What holds galaxies together?

Astronomers differ on explanations for Rubin's data. Galaxies may operate under laws that we have not yet discovered. We may not really understand the way gravity behaves with galaxies. Or there may be a great deal of mass in the universe that is unseen and unidentified, mass dubbed dark matter.

Rubin believes that we don't need any new theories. She still believes that gravity controls the movement of galaxies. Since calculations show that there is not enough gravity present to keep the outer stars from flying away, she theorizes that some invisible matter must be producing that gravitational force.

Many theories exist about what the dark matter might be and how much of it there is. Rubin suspects it is common, ordinary matter — "cold planets, dead stars, bricks, or baseball bats," she said in an interview. Other cosmologists believe the solution to the gravity problem may be new and exotic matter. And some think the laws of physics may need to be rewritten.

*Rubin surrounded by her collection of old globes.*

Some theories assume enormous amounts of dark matter, as much as one hundred times the mass of all the visible matter in the universe. That is ten times more mass than Rubin's own theory needs to keep spiral galaxies from flying apart. She thinks we see about ten percent of the Milky Way's matter on a starry night. Other astronomers think we may see only one percent. Since our galaxy contains around a hundred billion stars, holding it together would require a great deal of dark matter.

Whatever the material is that keeps galaxies from flying apart, the questions generated by Rubin's research will confound and delight astronomers for years to come. "With over ninety percent of the matter in the universe still to play with, even the sky will not be the limit," she says.

Vera Rubin faced many obstacles in becoming an astronomer, and she recognizes that women still struggle to be accepted. In addition to defending her own pioneering research, she has worked tirelessly to help women participate in science.

*Rubin with young women astronomers in the control room at Cerro Tololo. On her left is Wendy Freedman.*

Because she believes that knowing about other women scientists is important to girls deciding on careers, she has tried to improve the visibility of women astronomers.

In 1970, Rubin challenged plans for an exhibit at the Smithsonian Institution featuring advances in astronomy in the previous hundred years. In all the photos and memorabilia, there was not one picture, or even one mention, of a woman astronomer. Even Maria Mitchell, the most famous astronomer in America for a time, was not pictured.

When Rubin protested, she was told that planning for the exhibit was too far along to change. We can only hope her effort will mean oversights like this will not happen again.

*The Rubin family in the Rockies, around 1962. As grown-ups, sons Allan and David have PhDs in geology; Judith is an astronomer with a PhD in cosmic-ray physics; Karl has a PhD in mathematics.*

Unlike many women astronomers, Vera Rubin has enjoyed the support of a devoted husband and the rewards of raising four talented children. In describing the joy and fulfillment a career in science can bring, Rubin tells about a dinner conversation when the children were young. Ten-year-old Allan asked, "Do they pay you for the work you do at Carnegie?" Rubin added, "That made me realize he didn't know many people that had as much fun as I seemed to be having and were paid for doing it."

Vera Rubin personifies the trials and triumphs faced by women in science. She has pioneered new ways of thinking about how galaxies behave. Yet she has struggled all along for professional respect and credibility.

She must have been pleased with a telegram she received in 1978 that reads, "Dear Madame, You might appreciate hearing that four women astronomers are observing on Cerro Tololo tonight on the four largest telescopes! We are M.H. Ulrich, M.T. Ruiz, P. Lugger and L. Schweitzer." To which Rubin replied, "I hope the sky was very clear that night." ◉

*"I hope the sky was very clear that night."*

*A rare conjunction, or line-up, of the Moon, the planet Venus, the bright star Spica, and planet Jupiter (top to bottom) over Cerro Tololo, September 2005.*

# Exhilarating Discoveries, Painful Decisions

By 1940, some astronomers theorized that there were as many galaxies in the universe as there were stars in our own Milky Way galaxy. Beatrice Tinsley single-handedly developed the science of the birth, evolution, and death of galaxies.

*She showed a degree of mastery [understanding galactic evolution] that no one else before or since has attained.*

Sandra Faber, astronomer

## BEATRICE HILL TINSLEY

born 1941

died 1981

Beatrice Hill's pregnant mother couldn't sleep. The family had all heard the German bomb screaming down out of the dark sky. But they hadn't heard it explode. Now a live bomb lurked somewhere behind the garden fence. Nothing could be done until daylight, when the bomb squad could defuse it. Until then, Jean, Edward, and one small daughter huddled in their icy house.

Early the next morning, on a snowy January day, Beatrice, the second of three daughters, made her appearance. She was so premature that the doctor told her father to "not expect a live baby." Tiny Beatrice was very fragile, but she surprised them all. Her chances for survival grew when the family's hired man combed the neighborhood with a bucket, begging for coal to warm the bedroom enough to save the new baby.

Though the small town of Chester was not a primary military target, it was close enough to the manufacturing centers of Liverpool to get a frightening number of alerts and explosions. Enemy bombers often targeted a railroad yard behind the Hills' home, and explosions often damaged the ceilings and walls in the house.

When the war ended, Beatrice's parents emigrated to New Zealand. Her father wanted to become a minister in the Anglican Church, and he thought a career change would be easier in a new environment. Her

*Bombed-out buildings and debris, a typical sight in every city in England during the war.*

mother needed to live in a warmer, drier climate. They also wanted their children to grow up in a social atmosphere that was less class-oriented than that of Britain.

Beatrice flourished in the New Zealand school system, especially in math and music. Even as a small child, she was focused and industrious. Each week, she wrote a schedule for herself. She labeled every hour of every day with specific activities: piano practice, homework, and play time. She wrote letters to friends and family and kept a journal from a very early age.

In a letter home, Jean Hill described a scene she witnessed:

*Beatrice propped her stuffed koala bear Bruce up on the chair and picked up her violin. "The next item will be a violin solo," she announced. "The soloist will be Beatrice Hill. The pianist will be someone no one has heard of."*

*When the solo was over, Beatrice and Bruce bent over the small box that she was fashioning into a stringed instrument. Carefully, she wrapped rubber bands around the pegs she had mounted on the ends of the box. She hummed to herself as she plucked each "string" with the top of a metal clothes hanger and tightened the pegs until the band sounded the right note.*

Ten-year-old Beatrice studied music in school and at home, playing piano and violin. She instructed fuzzy Bruce in music theory and math exercises. She loved music nearly as much as she would grow to love mathematics.

By her junior year, Beatrice had mastered all the math available at the New Plymouth Girls High School. When she wanted to enter a competition in mathematics, she had to attend math classes at the Boys High School across town, because advanced math was only available for boys.

Beatrice entered Canterbury University in 1958, torn between majoring in math or physics. She finally decided on physics since "theoretical physics is mostly advanced maths anyway."

She didn't abandon music, however. Choosing the violin as her primary instrument, she searched out every opportunity to play. She filled her years at Canterbury with nearly equal parts science and music. She played violin with two different groups — the University Orchestra and the National Youth

## The Great Nebula Debate

Early astronomers saw thousands of fuzzy blobs in the night sky, and argued for centuries about what those fuzzy blobs might actually be. They called them nebulae, meaning misty or foggy. Some astronomers thought they were distant groups of stars and called them island universes. Others thought they were clouds of dust inside the Milky Way.

In 1920, the National Academy of Sciences sponsored a public debate between Harlow Shapley, who believed nebulae were dust clouds, and Heber Curtis, who thought they might be distant galaxies. Each debater had to address the same observations and describe the way those observations supported his position. The judges declared Shapley the winner and concluded that the existence of other galaxies outside our Milky Way was unlikely.

Improved telescopes have shown that each man was partly right. Some nebulae are dust clouds, some are galaxies, and some are objects no one had dreamed of — glowing gas clouds or enormous clusters of stars, called globular clusters.

*Orion Nebula*

Orchestra of New Zealand. In a letter she wrote to her parents, she said, "I'm terribly lucky aren't I?—this is really a wonderful life, full of science and labs and music."

Outstanding student that she was, Beatrice still loved a good party. Her picture as a debutante shows a cheerful, excited young woman ready to dance. One enthusiastic letter home describes the night she learned to swing dance.

Her regular letters kept her family up to date on all her academic and social activities. In one she wrote about her academic plans. "Instead of just sticking to the syllabus work in Chem and Physics, I'm reading and learning as much as I can about everything." Her enthusiasm about all facets of science helped lay the basis for her later productivity as a researcher in astronomy.

In 1961, Beatrice finished her first degree in physics, with an emphasis on cosmology, the study of the universe, or cosmos. She advanced quickly to a Master of Science degree, researching crystal structure. Before she began that course, however, she married Brian Tinsley, a fellow student who was finishing a PhD degree in physics and cosmology.

In 1963, the couple moved to Dallas, Texas, where Brian had accepted a position at the Southwest Center for Advanced Studies (SCAS), which later became the University of Texas at Dallas. Beatrice had a small research grant that SCAS was to administer, so she could continue her research. In a letter home, she predicted she and Brian would not stay in Texas for long.

By the end of the year, Tinsley knew she had to work more in astronomy if she was to be happy. The administration of SCAS considered women incapable of

***Sandra Faber*** helped discover scaling laws, important galactic features that let astronomers make more accurate predictions. The Faber-Jackson law correlates the size of a galaxy with the speed with which the stars in the galaxy move. Faber helped design the Hubble Space Telescope and was one of the team that diagnosed the Hubble's problem and designed a repair strategy. Her team identified the Great Attractor, a supercluster of galaxies that seems to attract everything, including the Milky Way, in a large region of space. It was this attraction that Vera Rubin was studying before she abandoned the research because of the controversy her data caused.

Spiral Galaxy

doing rigorous scientific work. They made it clear there were no positions for her there. The social scene was equally restricted. She regularly offended the faculty wives when she spent evenings talking science with the husbands rather than socializing with the wives.

The University of Texas at Austin had an astronomy program, however, led by a well-respected researcher. Despite the four-hundred-mile round trip, Tinsley enrolled in the PhD program. She stayed in Austin four days a week and in Dallas the other three. Meanwhile, her husband traveled widely, installing the solar spectrometers he designed and built.

Their busy schedules meant their time together was limited, even for people who needed little sleep. In a letter home, Tinsley wrote about Brian, "Last night I went out and left him there [on the roof of the physics building with his spectrometer] then drove to the Ozvaths and played sonatas, came home and worked for several hours, slept for two, and went and fetched B. when he rang up at 4 a.m."

In her work, Tinsley put together all the available information on the evolution of stars as a way to understand how galaxies evolve. For someone who read and absorbed everything she could find on chemistry, physics, and astronomy, the topic was a natural choice. She combined information about stellar evolution, stellar atmospheres, interstellar mediums, and the evolution of galaxies. She designed computer

Dwarf Galaxy

models to help her formulate theories about the way galaxies develop. Then, she devised more computer programs to model her theories.

Beatrice came to two major conclusions: First, the color of a galaxy depends on the way the stars in it were formed, and it changes over time. Second, because galaxies change in brightness as they evolve, astronomers who didn't take the changes into account introduced serious errors into their calculations when they used a galaxy as a standard for brightness.

In 1965, the Tinsleys adopted a baby boy. Two years later, Tinsley was awarded a PhD from the University of Texas. The following year, they adopted a baby girl. For the next ten years Tinsley managed her household and raised the children. She was active in organizations committed to social change, such as Planned Parenthood and Zero Population Growth. She was also a very busy astronomer.

Ring Galaxy

As a theoretical cosmologist, Tinsley analyzed the data produced by other astronomers and physicists. She thought about the way galaxies are born, grow old, and die. She believed that astronomers would not begin to understand the universe until they understood the evolution of galaxies. Working from home, she began her enormous output of publications on the evolution of galaxies.

Cluster Galaxy

People with Tinsley's abilities are called synthesists. They draw on their knowledge of a wide variety of disciplines to analyze information, make correlations, see patterns, and develop theories. Synthesists see the way information fits together.

Tinsley initiated many collaborative projects with other astronomers and quickly won their respect and admiration. As her reputation grew, she

Colliding Galaxies

was in increasing demand as a speaker at conferences and seminars. She was appointed visiting professor at the California Institute of Technology, the University of Maryland, the University of Texas at Austin, Lick Observatory, and Yale University. One friend called her the "Whole Earth Catalog of galactic studies," saying she knew everyone and everything going on in the field. A life-long prolific letter writer, she corresponded with astronomers, stargazers, and friends around the world.

Despite her growing professional stature, neither the University of Texas at Dallas nor Austin valued her contributions enough to offer her a job. She was hired to develop an astronomy course at Austin, but not allowed to teach it. In a letter to her father, she wrote:

Trying to work at U.T.D. reduced me to a state of mental anguish. Hard to explain! I am a good scientist, and among my peers treated like a full and respectable person and feel of worth. U.T.D. has kept me at the nearest possible level to nothing and there is no one who knows enough about astronomy to care in the least for my work. Austin has helped, but it is a second rate job, underpaid, half-time, at a department much worse than I'm worth. This isn't supposed to be boasting. To be rejected and undervalued intellectually is a gut problem to me, and I've lived with it most of the time we've been here.

Early in her time at Canterbury University, Tinsley had written in a letter, "One thing I certainly know, because I'm a woman my home must come before my science. That is right and it must be so and it would be unbearable otherwise. How bleak and bare life would be."

Seventeen years later, her girlish view of the world seemed hopelessly naive. Now she faced a wrenching decision. Her husband wouldn't leave

Texas, but she could not find work as an astronomer anywhere in the state. Knowing that it would mean leaving her family, Tinsley made the difficult decision to apply for a full-time position at Yale, in New Haven, Connecticut.

Rather than attempt a commuter marriage, virtually unknown at the time, Beatrice and Brian divorced. She did not want to uproot the children from their friends or neighborhood where they had grown up. So she granted legal custody of the children to their father. Despite the divorce, Tinsley remained devoted to her children, spending all her vacations with them. The entire family often traveled together to visit friends and family.

At Yale, Tinsley's productivity and reputation achieved new heights. She organized a hugely successful conference, "The Evolution of Galaxies and Stellar Populations." She traveled widely, speaking both to astronomers and to the public. She started weekly lunches for faculty and students, and she wrote scientific papers and, of course, letters.

In 1978, Tinsley was promoted to full professor at Yale, a remarkable achievement in just three years. Then, a few days after her promotion, she learned she had melanoma, a particularly virulent form of cancer. She had just a short time to live.

Tinsley rapidly recovered emotionally from this shattering news, and the next three years were as productive as any. Even in the hospital, during her final stay, Tinsley drafted one last paper for publication. She wrote it

## Tinsley as Synthesist

Synthesists see connections. They recognize the ways different pieces of data relate to each other. The best known scientific synthesists are James Watson and Francis Crick, who used other people's data to build a model of a DNA molecule. Watson and Crick's model fit the existing data and allowed scientists to see how such a molecule might replicate itself.

Beatrice Tinsley did not collect data directly from telescopes or other instruments. She studied published and unpublished information from astronomers and physicists, and used her understanding of chemistry, physics, and astronomy to develop theories about how stars are born, mature, and die. Then she used this life history of stars to make computer models of the ways entire galaxies of stars evolve. Synthesists are rare, even among scientists, and their skill often produces groundbreaking ideas, such as Tinsley's models of galactic evolution.

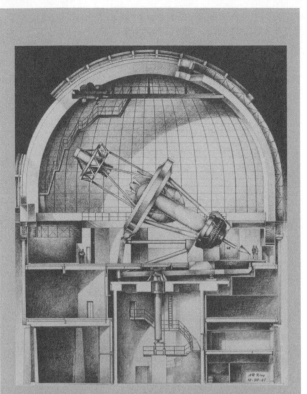

*The Mayall four-meter telescope, completed in late 1970, is the largest optical telescope on Kitt Peak in southern Arizona. Boasting a five-hundred-ton dome and a double shell structure, the telescope is designed to withstand hurricane force winds. The telescope has helped astronomers to study dark matter and the structure of elliptical galaxies, which in turn helps them understand the evolution of those galaxies.*

with her left hand because her right side had become paralyzed.

Beatrice Tinsley was an outstanding cosmologist and scholar. She wrote or collaborated on nearly one hundred scientific publications. Almost all came out in the fourteen years between completing her PhD, in 1967, and her death, in 1981. She was the first person to produce computer-generated models of how the color and brightness of galaxies change as the stars in them are born, grow old, and die.

Her work convinced astronomers that their practice of using galaxies as unvarying standards of brightness introduced large errors into their work. Galaxies evolve, she believed, just as the stars in them do. Their brightness changes during their evolution. This remarkable woman established the photometric evolution of galaxies as a separate field of study in astronomy.

Despite their refusal to hire her during her lifetime, the University of Texas at Austin created the Beatrice M. Tinsley Visiting Professorship in astronomy in her honor.

Tinsley was especially encouraging and supportive of astronomy students. In her obituary of Beatrice Tinsley, astronomer Linda Stryker says, "Young astronomers anywhere in the world might receive a letter from Beatrice commending them for a piece of work and urging them to continue their efforts." ◉

Telescopes that detect electromagnetic radiation in all regions of the spectrum allow astronomers to study all of a star's radiant output. These telescopes have led to the discovery of stars that emit almost no visible light. Jocelyn Bell discovered one of the first of these stars while still a graduate student at Cambridge.

*Obviously we were dealing with some sort of very rapidly rotating star."*

Jocelyn Bell

# S. JOCELYN BELL BURNELL

## born 1943

Jocelyn Bell couldn't believe the terrible news. How could she have failed such an important exam? Like her classmates, she'd been nervous. But that was to be expected. The test they all took at the end of their sixth year separated the students who would go on to study at Britain's universities from those who would be sent to trade schools.

How could she face her friends at the Armagh Observatory? She'd talked so often with them about her plans to be an astronomer. And her parents? Her architect-father had even designed parts of the observatory where she'd spent so many happy hours. Now it looked as if she'd never study astronomy, but would spend her life serving tea and scones to ladies in print dresses out for a day of shopping.

Jocelyn needn't have worried. Her parents knew how bright she was. They realized she had been poorly prepared by their local schools, and quickly arranged for her to attend a Quaker boarding school in England. The next time she took the test, she aced it. "Going to boarding school gave me a new start. It was a good idea and I did very well," she said years later in an interview.

*The Armagh Observatory in Ireland. Jocelyn Bell regularly visited this observatory near her home.*

The discoverer of pulsars was born Susan Jocelyn Bell, in Belfast, Northern Ireland, in 1943. Like many early women scientists, such as Maria Mitchell and Annie Cannon, Jocelyn grew up in a Quaker family. The children were taught to think for themselves and explore the world around them. As a child, Jocelyn rejected stereotypes. She built elaborate houses and even cars for her dolls, as well as styling their hair and sewing their clothes.

Passing the exam qualified her to attend a university. But her decision to major in physics kept her on the social fringe. When she entered the University of Glasgow, in Scotland, Jocelyn met the chilly reception common for women science majors of the time. "I was the only woman left in the physics class by the end of the first year," she said. Even her fellow students treated her as if she were "Jocelyn from Jupiter." But she stuck to her dream and

timeline continued
from page 88

1960

1961

Roman becomes Chief of Astronomy and Astrophysics at NASA.    Beatrice Hill marries Brian Tinsley in New Zealand.

graduated from Glasgow with honors in 1965.

When she entered Cambridge for graduate study in astronomy, Jocelyn Bell worked with astronomers doing the first research in radio astronomy, studying the radio waves emitted by stars. She helped design and build a telescope that focused on the radio waves emitted by objects in deep space. Professor Anthony Hewish, who had discovered that quasars could be detected by the "twinkle" produced when their light was influenced by the sun's solar wind, supervised her research.

Graduate students frequently built their own equipment. Bell, along with four other students, spent two years pounding about a thousand tall poles into the ground, then stringing miles of wire and cable from post to post. The array covered more than four acres and looked like an enormous basket. Students called it a four-and-one-half-acre telescope.

*The four-and-a-half acre telescope erected by Jocelyn Bell and her fellow graduate students. The poles are strung with cable to form an enormous radio receiver.*

With Bell supervising its operation, the radio telescope was first turned on in July 1967. The radio waves detected by the telescope were converted into electrical signals and recorded by pens moving over paper charts on long rolls. The recorders produced eight-inch-wide strips of graph paper that looked like EKG traces. Every day the telescope produced four hundred feet of paper with three tracks of data. Besides supervising the operation of the telescope, Bell analyzed the traces on miles of paper. First she had to eliminate those signals she could identify,

Rubin moves to Department of Terrestrial Magnetism at Carnegie Institution.

ruling out radio waves from human-made sources. Those included television broadcasts, aircraft altimeters, and the so-called pirate radio stations off the coast of Europe. Then she studied the remaining radio waves recorded by the telescope.

The radio telescope was designed specifically to spot Hewish's quasars, or quasi stellar objects. Bell and Hewish hoped they might identify radio waves from distant galaxies.

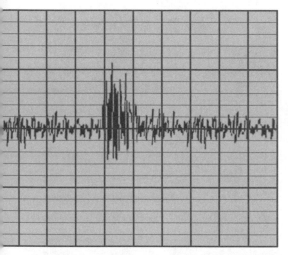

*An approximation of the chart paper with radio waves and the pulsar's "bit of scruff" that Bell noticed in August 1967.*

Bell looked at thousands of feet of paper and computed the time between certain peaks, as well as the wavelength of the detected radio waves. By the time the radio telescope had been running for three months, she was one thousand feet of chart paper behind. In another month, she was a third of a mile behind the recorder.

One day Bell noticed a strong signal that seemed to show up periodically. It appeared and disappeared regularly. She called it a "bit of scruff," but remembered she had seen it before. Her calculations told her this signal was coming from deep space, where the quasars should be.

The behavior of the signal, however, was all wrong. It seemed to turn on, then turn off, the way light from a lighthouse does. That suggested that the source was rotating. Bell knew that quasars don't rotate.

Professor Hewish thought Bell had detected some sort of human-made interference. No astronomer had ever detected a deep-space object that rotated every one and one-third seconds and emitted powerful radio waves.

Bell continued to search the charts for other "bits of scruff" and found two more in different spots in the sky. For a few days, Bell and Hewish wondered if these pulses could be from other planets. Perhaps some other civilization was trying to signal

## 1965

Jocelyn Bell earns doctorate from Cambridge University.

Earth. They jokingly began to refer to the source of the pulses as LGMs, or Little Green Men. But they seriously wondered what they'd found.

When she found three more sources, Bell began to think it was unlikely that civilizations on several distant planets would all try to contact Earth with exactly the same sort of radio signal. The media fixation with aliens became an annoying distraction. "Here am I trying to get a PhD out of a new technique and some silly lot of Little Green Men have to choose *my* frequency and *my* aerial to try signaling us," she laughed. But she realized that she had found an important new phenomenon.

Discovery of this totally new kind of star rocked the world of astronomy. Theories of star formation and evolution did not include stars that emitted such enormous energy while spinning so fast. No one had previously detected such a thing, and many astronomers were reluctant to rework their theories. The public, however, was delighted.

Enchanted with the possibility that a pretty twenty-four-year-old woman might have discovered the first evidence of extraterrestrial life, the media snapped picture after picture of her, sitting, standing, leaning, reading. They asked silly personal questions, such as "Are you taller or shorter than Princess Margaret?" and "How many boyfriends do you have?"

A reporter first named the radio stars pulsars, for Pulsating Radio Stars. Astronomers now believe that pulsars are rapidly rotating neutron stars. They form when a large star burns up all its hydrogen fuel and collapses in on itself. The resulting explosion, called a supernova, blows away most of the star.

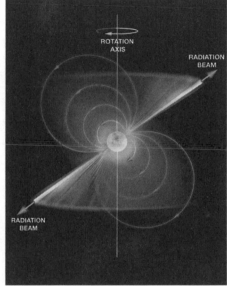

A pulsar is the small super dense core left after a massive star explodes in a supernova. Pulsars spin rapidly, emitting powerful bursts of electromagnetic radiation at regular intervals.

1967

Bell discovers pulsars. Tinsley earns doctorate in astronomy from University of Texas at Austin.

## The Society of Friends

The *Society of Friends*, usually called *Quakers*, was founded by George Fox in England in the seventeenth century. Fox believed that there was "that of God in every man" and rejected the idea of a rigidly structured church dominated by an educated clergy.

Fox's ideas were adopted differently by different groups of Quakers. Some *meetings*, as groups of Quakers call themselves, hold silent gatherings where each member worships according to his or her own design. Other meetings include speakers, and most encourage members to speak up during worship services.

Quakers have been a driving force in many civil and political changes. They were active in the effort to abolish slavery in the United States. They have worked for the rights of Native Americans.

Quakers believe strongly in the equal education of men and women. To support their belief in the rights of women to quality education, the Quakers established Bryn Mawr College, in 1885. Many outstanding women in history were raised in Quaker families.

Only the inner, remarkably dense core remains. This core is the equivalent of all the matter contained in our Sun, squashed into a ball just six miles wide.

Some astronomers think Bell's discovery of pulsars was one of the most important astronomical discoveries of the century. British astronomer Fred Hoyle said:

> There has been a tendency to misunderstand the magnitude of Miss Bell's achievement, because it sounds so simple — just to search and search through a great mass of records. The achievement came from a willingness to contemplate as a serious possibility a phenomenon that all past experience suggested was impossible.

Jocelyn Bell and Anthony Hewish received the Albert A. Michelson Medal for the discovery of pulsars. She was the first woman to be awarded the Beatrice M. Tinsley Prize by the American Astronomical Society. The Royal Astronomical Society presented

Geller graduates from UC Berkeley, receives NSF grant for graduate work.

her with the Herschel Medal in 1989. However, it was Hewish, not Bell, who was awarded the Nobel Prize in 1974 for the discovery of pulsars. Bell insisted she did not deserve the prize, that it was given for a lifetime of achievement, not a one-time discovery. Numerous astronomers disagreed and believed she should have at least shared the prize.

Shortly after receiving her PhD, Jocelyn Bell married and changed her name to Burnell. She began to move around England, following her husband as he advanced in his career in government service. For the next eighteen years, she took part-time, temporary jobs teaching astronomy and working in various astronomy and physics positions around England. She did not hold a full-time position until after she and her husband divorced.

In 1991, Jocelyn Bell Burnell was hired to teach astronomy in Britain's Open University, her first full-time job in twenty years. "Working at the Open University is very rewarding," she said. "I've had students on oil rigs, and lighthouse keepers. I'm impressed and sobered at the very able students who work evenings for a degree for six or eight years." For Bell Burnell, whose early second chance to retake an important exam launched her career in astronomy, it is important to see that other people also have a second chance at an education.

Bell Burnell continues to serve as a role model for women. When she was appointed Professor of Physics at the Open University, she became only the second woman in that position. She now chairs the Physics Department of the Open University, and has received many awards, including the Commander of the British Empire, for her service to astronomy. Jocelyn Bell Burnell's discovery of pulsars was one of the most exciting astronomical discoveries in the last half of the twentieth century. ◉

1971

Burbidge becomes director of Royal Greenwich Observatory.

Taken with the Wilson 24-inch reflector in Ireland, and scanned from original glass plates. Smudges and other defects are due to deterioration of the original glass plates.

1897

One hundred years of improving telescopes. The M51 nebula system is the first clearly recognized nebula system. It is about 31 million light-years away and is over 65,000 light-years across. These three images show the improvement in telescopes and detectors over the years.

Taken at Kitt Peak with the 0.9-meter telescope.

1991

Taken with the Hubble Space Telescope.

2005

As astronomers began to accept the theory that our universe started with a Big Bang, they also assumed that such a Big Bang would have spread matter evenly throughout that universe. When Margaret Geller's team discovered a pattern to the distribution of galaxies, it made scientists re-think that assumption.

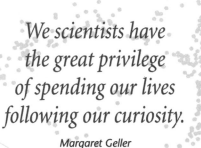

*We scientists have the great privilege of spending our lives following our curiosity.*

Margaret Geller

# MARGARET GELLER

### born 1947

On a warm summer day in 1985, Margaret Geller's graduate student spread out the map she had made of more than a thousand galaxies. As Geller looked at the first computer-generated picture of the positions of distant galaxies, she was flabbergasted. The map showed galaxies arranged in a structure Geller compared to the surface of soap bubbles, or the walls of honey combs. The galaxies seemed to form the walls of enormous cells, with nothing but empty space inside.

Margaret wasn't the only one to be flabbergasted — no one else had expected to find an overall structure to the universe, either. Most astronomers believed that galaxies were evenly spread throughout the universe. The discovery that the universe has a structure was so exciting that mapping the universe is now Margaret Geller's passion.

Margaret's parents, Seymour and Sarah Geller, read to her from the time she was a tiny baby. She grew up curious about the world around her, and her parents encouraged her quest to know about everything. They taught her algebra when she was just a small child and made sure she had many new books to read.

School in Morristown, New Jersey, was not a pleasant experience for Margaret. It was boring and oppressing, and she frequently pretended to be sick so she could stay home. When her parents figured out what she was doing, they said she could skip school, provided that she study hard at home.

That arrangement helped, but school remained a problem. One of Margaret's teachers publicly ridiculed her for being shy and awkward. This same teacher then told her that women did not do science and that she should forget about math and science classes. Her father countered that message by taking her to work with him. He was an X-ray crystallographer at Bell Labs. He put her to work measuring wavelengths and distances on X-ray diffraction photographs. Those are pictures of X-rays bouncing off atoms in a crystal. The distances between atoms can be measured from the photos. Margaret entered the numbers into a "wonderful old mechanical calculator, which would bang and thump mightily as it ground through the calculations." Other scientists and engineers stopped by constantly. And Margaret learned that even shy girls merited respect and friendship.

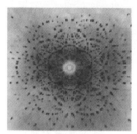

X-ray diffraction pattern of the mineral beryllium aluminum silicate, or emerald.

The early 1950s were exciting times to be at Bell Labs. Some scientists worked on the first laser technology, while others developed applications for transistors. Fifty years later, lasers guide jet planes and help surgeons repair nerve tissue. Transistors led to personal computers, global positioning, and iPods. Even a

1973

child could feel the excitement that surrounded the work at Bell Labs. "I got the idea that science was an exciting thing to do and there were people who really enjoyed doing it, and that it could be rewarding," Geller said.

During high school, Geller indulged her love of language. She entered state competitions in poetry reading and debate, and played the lead in many high-school plays. She enjoyed drama so much she persuaded her parents to send her to acting school.

After high school, Geller attended the University of California at Berkeley, where she majored in physics. When she graduated, in 1970, she received a National Science Foundation fellowship for graduate study in physics at Princeton University. She planned to study solid-state physics, the foundation of transistor and silicon chip technology, but her advisor talked her out of it. He said the field was mature, and few new developments were expected. Taking his advice, Geller switched her major to astrophysics.

Geller's experience at Princeton was in some ways a repeat of her elementary school days. Princeton had been accepting women for just a few years, and many faculty and students resented the presence of women on campus, especially in science. Despite the cold environment for women at Princeton, Margaret persevered. In 1975, she earned her PhD, the second woman to earn a doctorate in physics from Princeton. She took a job at the Harvard-Smithsonian Center for Astrophysics.

Three years later, as a visiting professor at Cambridge University, in England, Geller's self-confidence hit bottom. The hostility at Princeton had shaken her, and she realized that if she planned to continue doing astrophysics, she needed to develop a focus to her research.

*Amy Barger,* at the University of Hawaii, searches for distant galaxies. With a new telescope that detects light in very long wavelengths, Barger and her team have discovered many galaxies hidden behind dust clouds.

*Gwen Bell* looked for new ways to calculate the mass of the Milky Way while she was still a student at Harvey Mudd. She worked at the U.S. Naval Observatory at Flagstaff, Arizona, during the summers. For her efforts, Bell received the $6,000 Leroy Apker Award for Undergraduates. She also received accolades from other astronomers. Andrea Ghez said, "I think she did a beautiful piece of work."

1974

Geller said:

***Jane Luu*** was lucky to get a spot on one of the last cargo planes out of South Vietnam as the American forces left and the North Vietnamese army poured into Saigon. Twelve years later, Luu was a graduate student in planetary astronomy at MIT. Here she searched the skies for a source of comets known as the Kuiper Belt. The belt was named after the astronomer who theorized its existence. By 1995, Luu had found evidence of the comet source.

> I decided that now was the time to put up or shut up — that if I wasn't going to make a really serious commitment to the field, I might as well get out. And if I was going to be in science, the exciting thing was to be out there. I began to think about what was known concerning the large-scale structure of the universe. I realized that, in fact, very little was known for sure. People were generalizing from a severely limited number of observations. I recognized just how fragile were the foundations of the field. And when I returned to Harvard, John [Huchera] and I sat down and mapped out a long-term research effort aimed at getting at these issues.

When she returned to the Harvard-Smithsonian Center, Geller began to study the way galaxies were distributed in the universe. She used a telescope fitted with a spectroscope to measure the redshift of distant galaxies, the same process Edwin Hubble had used in 1929. The redshift can be used to calculate how far the galaxy is from the Earth, and how fast it is receding from the Earth (see page 134).

In 1929, Hubble's equipment was so slow that he had to spend a full night to record the redshift from just one galaxy. Now, Geller and her team can take data from nearly five hundred galaxies in a single night.

Geller's first hint about a possible structure to the universe came in the early 1980s. She and her team, however, decided these first data did not describe true structures. The idea was so much at odds with the existing assumptions about the universe that they thought there must have been some kind of error. But Geller

## Margaret Geller Talks to Students

It was my father who showed me the exquisite beauty of having an explanation for something we observe in nature. It is that aesthetic of science which has, I think, kept me doing it in spite of some rather severe frustrations.

My first piece of advice to any young person is: "Do something you love." The natural question is then, I suppose, "Why should I love Science?"

I suppose that for me the greatest pleasure is the attraction to patterns in nature. I have always found them beautiful and somehow the pleasure in that beauty increases with deeper understanding. Of course, I have had the great gift of being the co-discoverer of the largest patterns in nature . . . the bubble-like structure defined by galaxies like our own Milky Way. The feeling that goes with this kind of discovery . . . the feeling of wonder and awe that you are the first to see a pattern in nature . . . is one you carry with you for your whole life. There is an internal and an external pleasure . . . the internal one comes from the satisfaction of solving a puzzle, the external one from sharing its beauty with others.

Major discoveries are rare in science, but there is an excitement in being part of the process of discovery. For being part of that process, there are a number of important skills and personality traits. I believe that mathematical and analytic skills are fundamental. Science today is increasingly technical. The more tools one brings to bear, the better.

Imagination coupled with a kind of courage is also important. Science at the forefront is a high risk, high gain endeavor . . . like all other creative professions, including the arts. Science is about making connections where there were none before. For that reason a broad education is as crucial as development of technical skill. Reading great literature, seeing art in all its forms, and internalizing them are challenges of understanding nature.

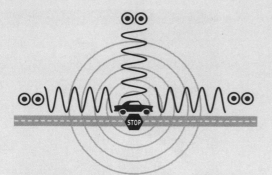

Stopped car sounds the same to everyone.

## Redshift

When we watch race cars on television, we notice the change in sound as a car hurtles by the camera. The pitch is higher as the car nears, then lower as the car recedes. This change in pitch is called the Doppler effect, named for the German scientist who first described it. The Doppler effect is caused by the sound waves compressed against the detector, our ear, as the car approaches, then stretched out as the car recedes.

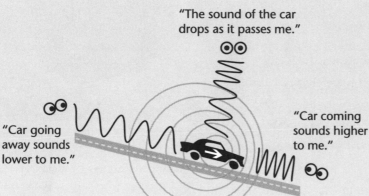

"The sound of the car drops as it passes me."

"Car going away sounds lower to me."

"Car coming sounds higher to me."

Light waves exhibit a Doppler effect too, though our eyes are not sensitive enough to detect it. The Doppler effect in light is called a redshift or blueshift. A light source moving toward you shifts toward the higher frequency, or blue end of the spectrum. A light source moving away shifts to a lower frequency and becomes redder.

"Light looks redder to me."

"Light looks bluer to me."

1975

was intrigued and suggested that her graduate student Valerie de Lapparent conduct a new survey for her thesis work.

In the summer of 1985, de Lapparent plotted the data from 1057 galaxies. The plot showed that the 1057 galaxies were nearly all arranged in thin walls surrounding vast empty spaces. When she saw this, Geller says, she was flabbergasted. She describes these enormous structures as being like soap bubbles in a sink full of suds. The galaxies are spread across the surface of the bubble, with nothing but vast, empty space inside.

Since publishing their data in 1986, Geller and her team continue to add to it and analyze their results. Each study seems to confirm their original finding: There is some enormous structure to the universe.

Geller, however, cautions that their sample is still small compared to the total universe. "Big as it is, our survey area compared with the visible universe is like Rhode Island compared with the surface of the Earth." So far Geller and her team have covered just one one-hundred-thousandth of the visible universe.

Ever since Edwin Hubble proposed that the universe originated with a Big Bang, astronomers have imagined that the blast resulted in a fairly even distribution of matter throughout

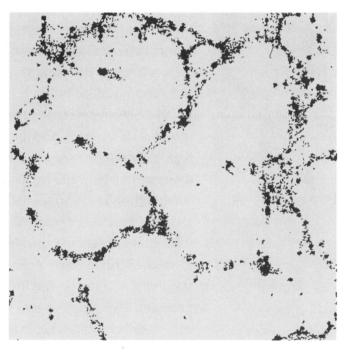

*Galaxies appear to clump together in filaments with large empty spaces between them, somewhat like soap bubbles. The spaces are almost completely empty — stray atoms are hundreds of miles apart.*

C. Shoemaker goes to work at USGS in Flagstaff, Arizona.          Ride receives PhD degree in astrophysics from UCLA.

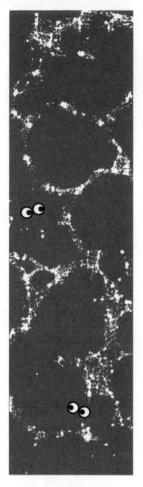

The soap-bubble universe appears to be large empty spaces surrounded by walls of superclusters of galaxies.

the universe. The idea of some overall structure in the universe came as a shock.

The results were so surprising that they triggered tremendous interest in a possible structure of the universe, and mapping it became a priority. Geller says mapping the universe also gives her something to say to people who ask her what she does. "Once I said I was a cosmologist, but I got asked about makeup. Now I say I make maps."

Geller believes the maps may hold important information of their own. "I often feel we are missing some fundamental element in our attempts to understand this structure," she says. "A lot of science is really the same as mapping. You have to make a map before you understand."

Geller believes the maps will help astronomers refine their questions about the early life of the universe: "Are the vast dark regions [voids] we see empty or are they full of mysterious dark matter? How did the pattern with sheets full of galaxies surrounding voids originate?"

In 1990, Geller received a MacArthur Fellowship. These fellowships are often called "genius" awards because they are given to highly creative people in all professions. They recognize the abilities of the person but are not given for a special research program. The recipient uses the money in any way she chooses.

Geller combines her interest in drama and literature with her concern about science education. She collaborated in the production of a forty-minute film, *So Many Galaxies ... So Little Time.* The film focuses on Geller and her team as they work through a typical day, wrapping up with an observing-night breakfast of watermelon and enchiladas. It ends with a spectacular computer-simulated flight through the stars and galaxies.

"All the science films I've seen, I've always asked myself, Where's the emotion? Where's the thrill? Where's the story?" Geller said. "I wanted to make a romantic movie about science." ◉

# Challenges for the 21st Century

Most late-twentieth-century astronomers gazed farther and farther out into the universe, but a few concentrated on residents of and visitors to our own solar system. Some were worried that the Earth could be on a collision course with an enormous chunk of rock, as they believed it had been in the past. Carolyn Shoemaker searches the skies for those rocks.

*Comets are the wild cards.*

Carolyn Shoemaker

Carolyn Shoemaker held her breath as an enormous chunk of comet slammed into Jupiter, gouging a gaping black wound in the planet's surface. All eyes in the room strained toward the television screen as nineteen more comet fragments pounded the planet, stitching a line of scars longer than the Earth is wide. If the Earth had been in the path of comet Shoemaker-Levy 9 on that July day in 1994, most life would have been destroyed, just as Carolyn Shoemaker believes that life on Earth has been destroyed before.

# CAROLYN SPELLMAN SHOEMAKER

**born 1929**

Carolyn Spellman didn't set out to be the woman who discovered that incredibly destructive comet, or the other thirty-two she has found. She grew up in New Mexico and in Chico, California, thinking that science was boring and scientists were all old men.

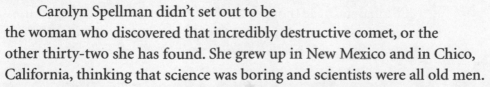

*In July, 1994, the comet Shoemaker-Levy 9 slammed into Jupiter, gouging great holes out of the planet and leaving behind black scars on the planet's surface.*

Instead of studying science, she earned degrees in history and political science from the University of California at Chico.

On graduating from college, Carolyn taught seventh grade for a short time, until she met Gene Shoemaker at her brother's wedding. Gene, a graduate student in geology, was her brother's best man and former college roommate. Friends and family rightly thought Carolyn and Gene were a good match, and they married in 1951. Carolyn left teaching and became a stay-at-home mom, raising three children.

In 1976, with her children grown, Carolyn was ready for a new challenge. Gene suggested she work with him at the U.S. Geological Survey labs in Flagstaff, Arizona, where he needed additional staff. He thought she'd be interested in learning to use the telescope to search for near-Earth asteroids.

1978

Ride is among first women chosen by NASA to begin astronaut training.

Gene Shoemaker believed that meteors or comets had smashed into the Earth and annihilated the dinosaurs — along with much of the rest of life on Earth — at least once. He also thought it could happen again, and astronomers were paying far too little attention to that possibility. At the time, few people knew how many asteroids or comets might cross the path of Earth in the next year, let alone the next decade. Only a few brave souls would go as far as suggesting that Earth could actually be hit by an asteroid. Carolyn was interested in Gene's work and had traveled with him on his geological surveys. And so, in 1980, at age 51, Carolyn Shoemaker went to work searching for Earth-approaching asteroids.

Carolyn fell in love with astronomy. The woman who once thought that all astronomers were "old men in white beards, smoking pipes, and staring at the sky," discovered she had both the temperament and the eyesight to be a first-class comet finder. "I slid gradually into planetary astronomy as a field, while working on Gene's search program, and loved it for the opportunity to keep on learning new things each day. Of course, the thrill of discovery of both asteroids and comets gave me a deep satisfaction,"

## The Hubble Constant and the Age of the Universe

In 1929, Edwin Hubble noticed that the farther a galaxy was from Earth, the faster it was speeding away. He proposed a factor, now called the Hubble Constant, that related the speed of the galaxy to the age of the universe. His first estimates of the size of the factor, around 100, produced a startling contradiction — many stars appeared to be billions of years older than the universe itself.

The problem lured astronomers, who gathered data and recalculated the constant for decades. Each new calculation decreased the apparent error, but never quite enough. Precise data required an orbiting telescope, and the launch of the Hubble Space Telescope finally allowed the contradiction to be resolved.

In 1999, Wendy Freedman used data from the Hubble Space Telescope to recalculate the constant. The new value, well below 100, suggests a universe that is old enough — about twelve billion years old — to contain the oldest stars. The value also suggests that the universe may expand forever, and seems to support the Big Bang theory of formation.

1979

Cecilia Payne-Gaposchkin dies.

1981

Beatrice Tinsley dies.

she said in an interview.

Gene Shoemaker's conviction that a large asteroid slamming into the Earth had unleashed the cataclysmic changes that wiped out the dinosaurs was controversial for two reasons. First, there were no obvious craters on the Earth's surface that supported the theory. Second, few people believed that asteroid orbits brought them close enough to Earth to be a danger. In the course of their travels, the Shoemakers proved the doubters wrong on both counts, and established the field of impact geology.

They traveled the globe searching for large impact craters and have found enough evidence to convince most skeptics. Unfortunately, their travels also resulted in the death of Gene Shoemaker who, in 1997, was killed in an auto crash near Alice Springs, Australia. Carolyn was badly injured, but recovered and went back to searching for nearby asteroids and comets. She now works twelve- to thirteen-hour days. She estimates that she finds a new asteroid or comet about every one hundred hours.

Discovering the comet that smashed into Jupiter reinforced the Shoemakers' theory that impacts with Earth would have devastating consequences for life. "It was doubtless the most satisfying and significant achievement of my life in astronomy," Carolyn says. "Comets are the wild card when we consider the potential for impact on Earth. We cannot predict the coming of long-period comets well in advance, and it is necessary to learn more if we wish to defend our planet. We need to know a great deal more about their structure — are they solid bodies emitting gas and dust, or are they unconsolidated flying snowballs easily broken apart, or are they all shades in between?"

Carolyn herself has amassed convincing evidence of asteroids that could threaten Earth. At last count she had discovered thirty-two comets, including the spectacular Shoemaker-Levy 9, whose collision with Jupiter

***Heidi Hammel*** became a familiar media face when she led the team studying the collision of Comet Shoemaker-Levy 9 with Jupiter in 1994. Her enthusiasm and ability to explain complex concepts in simple terms made her popular with television viewers. Hammel is now a principal research scientist at MIT.

1983

Ride becomes first American woman in space, aboard the shuttle *Challenger*.

1985

Geller team observes large structure in universe.

## How Dangerous Are Asteroids?

Carolyn Shoemaker looks for asteroids that may threaten Earth. But how much of a threat is an asteroid? You can calculate the energy of an impact, the size of the hole an asteroid might gouge in the surface of the Earth, and whether or not people would be injured. Go to the web site developed by astronomers at the University of Arizona: http://www.jpl.arizona.edu/impacteffects. At the web site, you can enter information about a made-up asteroid and see the effect of an impact near you.

The asteroid that formed Wolfe Creek Crater (below) slammed into Western Australia 300,000 years ago. It would have sent tons of dust into the atmosphere, possibly influencing the weather all around Australia. The crater it left is 875 meters across and 60 meters deep.

Asteroid 243 Ida is about 56 kilometers long and travels in the asteroid belt between Mars and Jupiter. This photo was taken during the 1993 Galileo spacecraft flyby.

1986

Space shuttle *Challenger* explodes on lift-off, killing all seven astronauts aboard.

## Finding Comets and Asteroids with Photography

Carolyn Shoemaker and her husband, Gene, developed a stereo machine that lets a comet seeker use two photographs to find comets. Using the two photographs, taken from forty-five minutes to an hour apart, the researcher looks through a stereoscope designed so that one eye looks at one photo and the other eye looks at the other photo. The brain meshes the photographs together and superimposes the dot-like stars over each other.

Because comets and asteroids move more rapidly than stars appear to move, there will be a tiny distance between them on the photo. When the observer's brain puts them on top of each other, they look as if they are floating above the flat surface of the stars.

This combination of two photos, taken 109 minutes apart, illustrates how far the fateful comet SL-9 moved on the night Shoemaker discovered it.

In order to use the device effectively, researchers must have good stereo vision and be well trained. Carolyn Shoemaker is so skillful she spots about one comet or near-Earth object every one hundred hours.

demonstrated, for all the world to see, the devastation such collisions could cause. She has discovered more than three hundred asteroids, including forty Earth-approaching asteroids. As her search continues, her delight in discovery also continues. When she finds a comet, she says, "I want to dance. I usually go to the staircase and call up to the observers at the telescope and yell, 'Yay-y-y-y-y!'"

For her discoveries, Shoemaker was awarded the Rittenhouse Medal, as well as an honorary doctorate of science from Northern Arizona University. She became a Cloos scholar at Johns Hopkins University in 1990.

Carolyn Shoemaker continues to scan the skies, hoping to keep humans from meeting the fate of the dinosaurs. ◉

Bigger and better telescopes let astronomers see farther into the universe. But many people still yearned to experience first hand the wonders that lay beyond the Earth. Sally Ride was the first American woman to go into space.

*This is definitely an E-ticket ride.*

Sally Ride

# SALLY RIDE

**born 1951**

The measured tones of Mission Control sounded through Sally Ride's headset. "Three, two, one, ignition. We have ignition." A thunderous roar engulfed the small capsule, nearly drowning out the next words: "Lift off, we have lift off." For several minutes the vibration and roar of the enormous rockets battered the crew. Then the experience described by Ride as "bone rattling and mind numbing" ended, and the capsule detached from the engines to soar into orbit around the Earth. Thirty-two-year-old Sally Ride was on her way to space.

America's first woman in space was born in Los Angeles, California, six years before the beginning of the space race. At that time, only science-fiction writers and a few far-sighted researchers thought much about space flight. That changed when Sally Ride was six years old and Russia launched *Sputnik I*, the first earth-orbiting satellite. The race for space was on, and Sally Ride grew up

*The first men to land on the Moon drove the Lunar Rover around, collecting rocks and dust for study on Earth.*

with the American space program. After she became an astronaut, Sally said, "I've always watched the space program closely. I could tell you exactly where I was when John Glenn went into space and when Neil Armstrong walked on the moon."

In 1961, President John F. Kennedy pledged that the United States would put a man on the moon by 1970. Although she avidly followed the events in the space program, Sally knew the president really meant a *man* on the moon, not a woman on the moon. Women had little part in the early space program.

Dale and Joyce Ride, Sally's parents, were both teachers. They encouraged Sally and her younger sister, Karen, to explore all their physical and intellectual interests. As part of a lively, competitive family, Sally grew up learning the mental and physical skills required of an astronaut. She devoured adventure stories, especially Nancy Drew mysteries and science fiction.

Even as a small child, Sally loved sports. She read the sports page with her father and memorized baseball statistics when she was just five years old. She played baseball and football with the neighborhood kids, usually on the winning team. She even fantasized about becoming a major league baseball player. When her parents gently suggested that she learn to play tennis instead, she decided to become the best tennis player she could be.

1990                                                                                    1993

Geller receives MacArthur "genius" fellowship. NASA launches Hubble space telescope.          Helen Hogg dies.

While she perfected her tennis game, Sally took all the math and science classes she could. Her tenth-grade science teacher, Dr. Elizabeth Mommaerts, taught her the process of problem-solving through deductive reasoning. Sally's skill in problem-solving added to her enjoyment of chemistry, physics, trigonometry, and calculus, and helped her become a successful astronaut.

In high school, Sally was the eighteenth-ranked junior tennis player in the United States. She won the Eastern Intercollegiate Woman's Tennis Championships in both her first and second years at Swarthmore College, in Philadelphia. She then transferred to the University of California at Los Angeles.

At UCLA, Sally met Billie Jean King, the reigning American woman tennis champ, who encouraged her to become a professional athlete. Sally started an intense training program, but decided after several months that she would never be the champion tennis player she wanted to be. Giving up her goal of a career in professional tennis, she entered Stanford University, graduating in 1973 with a BA in English and a BS in physics. She immediately entered the Stanford graduate program in physics and astronomy, studying X-ray-emitting stars.

Four years later, when Ride was just about finished with her PhD in astrophysics, she saw a notice in the student newspaper. NASA was looking for scientists to become "mission specialists" for space shuttle flights. Better yet, and for the first time, women were invited to apply. In 1978, NASA chose thirty-five new astronauts to train, including six women. Sally Ride was one of them.

Her family was thrilled with the news. "I think my Dad was kind of happy when I became an astronaut," said Ride. "Before

*Eleanor (Glo) Helin* was principal investigator of the Near Earth Asteroid Tracking program of NASA's Jet Propulsion Laboratory, until her retirement in 2002. She discovered or co-discovered 863 asteroids, one of which, asteroid 3267 Glo, is named for her ("Glo" is her nickname).

*Lucy-Ann McFadden* is an astronomer and geophysicist who studies comets and asteroids. For two weeks every month during the dark of the moon, McFadden and her team scan for faint, fast-moving objects such as near-Earth asteroids. She has been the principal investigator of NASA's planetary geology program since 1984, and works at the California Space Institute at the University of California, San Diego.

1994

Comet Shoemaker-Levy collides with Jupiter.

*The first six women astronauts: Shannon Lucid, Margaret Rhea Seddon, Kathryn Sullivan, Judith Resnik, Anna Fisher, and Sally Ride.*

### Sandra Pizzarello

studies meteorites, looking for chemicals that might have clues to early life on Earth. In 1969, she found amino acids in a meteorite that landed in Australia. Laboratory tests showed the amino acids were active. The results supported Pizzarello's theory that meteorites influenced the way life developed on Earth.

I joined NASA, I was in theoretical astrophysics. Astronaut was a concept he understood."

Astronaut training began in 1979 at the NASA-Johnson Space Center in Clear Lake City, just south of Houston, Texas. Along with the rest of the class, the six women learned everything there was to know about their spacecraft. As the only people who would be there to fix problems that might come up in space, the trainees learned about the computer that helps operate the space shuttle. They learned about the shuttle's mechanical and electrical systems, and practiced handling failures of each system. And they learned how to eat, sleep, and exercise in space.

While they studied the shuttle, trainees learned how to survive being ejected from a jet plane, parachuting between electrical lines and through trees. They learned to fly in a T-38 jet trainer — the shuttle was a sort of airplane, after all. Ride enjoyed the flying so much she continued lessons and got her pilot's license.

American space shuttle launches take place over the open ocean, in the hope that astronauts can be rescued from the ocean if the shuttle has a problem. To practice being ejected from a damaged shuttle into the ocean, trainees endured an exercise called "drop and drag."

The exercise is designed to simulate being dragged through the water by a still-inflated parachute. Ride, dressed in a full flight suit and strapped into a parachute, was thrown from a moving boat and dragged through the ocean at high speed. She had to release herself from the parachute harness and swim to the dock.

Along with specific facts and skills, Sally and her classmates learned more computer science, math, and engineering. They each studied the specific tasks they would have as a mission specialist. Sally was trained in operating a mechanical arm called the remote manipulator system, or RMS. The manipulator lifts satellites in and out of the shuttle's cargo bay and is operated from inside the shuttle.

During her training time, Sally also met and married fellow astronaut Steve Hawley. They are now divorced.

**Anneila I. Sargent** directs the Owens Valley Radio Observatory for the California Institute of Technology. She helped discover the first planets outside our own solar system.

Finally, in 1981, Sally Ride was named mission specialist on the seventh shuttle mission of the Space Shuttle *Challenger*, scheduled for June, 1983. She was the first American woman, the first person who was not a military test pilot, and the youngest astronaut to go into space.

Ride's first shuttle mission attracted intense media attention. Astronauts are the human face of the space program, and Ride was well trained in public relations. She surely knew her smiling face crowned with curly brown hair would be on the front of every U.S. newspaper. She bore the media spotlight like a pro.

Reporters asked her silly questions: Would she wear a bra in space? Did she cry when she got angry? One reporter told the mission captain, Robert Crippen, that Texans didn't think a woman could do an astronaut's job. Crippen, a Texan himself, said, "I've found that all the women astronauts have carried their share and more. We work together as a unit, but the fact that one is male and one is female, I haven't found made one bit of difference."

*Mission-specialist Ride in the cabin of the space shuttle.*

As flight engineer, Ride assisted the commander and pilot during liftoff and landing. She monitored data from the computers and kept the pilot aware of the progress of the lift-off. If a problem arose, Ride had the responsibility of suggesting responses and solutions.

On June 18, 1983, the *Challenger* lifted off. As the crew reached orbit and settled down to their duties, Mission Control communicator Roy Bridges asked, "How is it up there?"

"Have you ever been to Disneyland, Roy?" Ride replied. "Well, this is definitely an 'E' ticket."

Ride's second shuttle mission came in October, 1984. This time she was joined by another woman, Kathryn Sullivan, a geologist with expertise in remote sensing equipment. On this mission, Sullivan would be the first American woman to walk in space.

For the next two years, Sally Ride worked and studied at NASA. She also traveled throughout the United States, speaking about the space program and receiving recognition for her achievement. She was awarded the Meridian Award, presented to individuals who have achieved high goals and made new strides

*The space shuttle in lift-off from Cape Canaveral. The shuttle, seen attached to the fuel tanks, will blow the tanks free with explosive bolts when the necessary altitude and speed are attained.*

in professional and personal endeavors. Ride was also presented with the Lindbergh Eagle Award by Anne Morrow Lindbergh, widow of Charles A. Lindbergh, the pilot who made the first solo flight across the Atlantic.

*The space shuttle in a glide path to a landing at Kennedy Space Center.*

In spite of her achievements and awards, Sally Ride's most difficult task was still ahead of her. As she drove to the space center in Houston on the morning of January 28, 1986, Ride listened to the countdown for the launch of the tenth *Challenger* mission. The voice from her radio must have seemed familiar, even comforting. "Four point three nautical miles, down range distance three nautical miles." Then the command, "*Challenger*, go with throttle up."

Seventy-three seconds into the flight, with the craft ten miles up, the *Challenger* exploded in a fiery ball of smoke and flames, killing all seven astronauts instantly. They had all been Ride's friends and colleagues, and Judy Resnik had been one of Ride's 1978 classmates.

Stunned as she was, Ride must have taken some comfort in knowing that the *Challenger* crew probably didn't even know what happened. "When I realized how fast it happened, I guess it sort of hit home to me that during launch that's not what you're thinking about," she said later.

With America in shock and the space program in shambles, President Reagan appointed a commission to investigate the cause of the disaster and recommend solutions. The only active astronaut on the commission was Sally Ride. Retired astronaut Neil Armstrong, the first person to walk on the moon, was vice-chairman.

The report produced by the investigating commission totaled 256 pages and pinpointed a number of safety problems at the space agency. Based on the report, the president stopped all space flights until the problems were solved.

**Alyssa Goodman,** at Harvard's Astronomy Department, studies dark clouds, huge, dusty places in space where stars are born. As a high school student, Goodman was torn between studying physics and anthropology because she found both fascinating. When she accepted an internship at the NASA-Goddard Institute for Space Studies, her future career was set.

Another four years would pass before the launch of another space shuttle. Ride was ready for new challenges and not willing to wait. She wrote and published a book for children called *To Space and Back*. She dedicated the book to her science teacher, Elizabeth Mommaerts, and to the memories of her fellow astronauts who were killed when the *Challenger* exploded.

Ride made an important final contribution to NASA when she became a part of the Long Range and Strategic Planning Department at NASA. She led a group of astronauts and scientists in studying the entire operation of NASA. A year and a half after the *Challenger* disaster, they produced *The Ride Report*, in which they suggested new directions for space exploration. One of Ride's suggestions, that astronauts participate in management decisions about shuttle launches, has resulted in improved safety.

When asked recently if she would go back to space, Ride answered, "If they asked me to go tomorrow, I'd say, 'Yes.' But if they said I'd have to train for two years first, I'd say, 'No thanks.'"

Ride returned to teaching and research in astrophysics. She was professor of physics and astrophysics, and director of the California Space Institute at the University of California at San Diego until 1996. Her research focused on space plasma physics and on natural laser processes.

In order to encourage girls to pursue science, math, and technology careers, Sally Ride established Sally Ride Science. The company publishes books about science and scientists, and hosts a web site club. It also offers summer camps at NASA facilities, and provides after-school programs for promising young scientists. ◉

**Movies and TV** series such as *Star Wars, Star Trek,* and *Babylon 5* contain some great special effects. They also contain many examples of bad science, scenes that defy the laws of physics. See if you can tell what is wrong in the scenes described below. Answers on the next page.

1. In the opening scene of *Babylon 5,* the viewer sees the space station from a distance. A roar in the background suggests the viewer hears the motors of the station. What is wrong with this scene?

2. Many science-fiction films and television series include an exciting chase through an asteroid field. The hero or heroine speeds between asteroids, barely escaping annihilation. The bad guys, of course, either give up or smash into an asteroid, blowing up their ship with colorful special effects. What fact of astronomy is ignored in these scenes?

3. In the opening scene of *Star Trek: The Next Generation*, viewers seem to move out through our solar system, enjoying beautiful views of the planets as they speed by. What's wrong with this picture?

4. Many science-fiction movies and television shows try to include as much science as they can. If the drama deals with space travel, however, various creative ideas are employed to avoid what many astronomers consider a physical law. Do you know what that law is and the ways writers get around it?

# Answers:

1. The scene ignores the fact that sound is produced by the compression and expansion of air. There is no air in space, so there can be no sound in space unless it is transmitted through some mechanical or electronic system.

2. The chase through the asteroid field suggests that asteroids are very close together. Philip Plait, writing in the December 1998 issue of *Astronomy* magazine, says asteroids are so far apart that "you could tool around out there for months and never see one asteroid, let alone, two." Plait maintains a web page for examples of bad astronomy in the movies and on TV.

3. Imagine standing on Earth with a telephoto lens aimed at Mars. A glance at a model of our solar system will show that the planets are spread all around you. They do not line up in such a photogenic manner.

4. To travel the vast distances involved, the characters would have to travel faster than light, which Einstein's equations seem to prohibit. Many scientists think that faster-than-light travel will never be possible. Stories that show a character traveling to the far side of the galaxy, millions of light years, assume that in the future we will have invented some form of travel beyond our current technology. To get around the speed limit, science-fiction script writers use a number of devices. The *Star Trek* series uses warp speeds, multiples of the speed of light. Viewers must take it on faith that warp engines somehow move the space ship many times faster than light. *Babylon-5* writers use jump gates to get around a cosmic speed limit. The gates take space ships into something called "hyper-space," some unexplained, and currently unknown, folding of space-time that shortens distances.

The movie *Contact* is unusually true to scientific principles. Astronomer Carl Sagan wrote the book, supervised the screen play, and made every attempt to keep the movie true to what we know about physics and astronomy. The movie includes scenes from the telescope at Arecibo, Puerto Rico, used for the search for extraterrestrial intelligent life.

Watching science-fiction television stories and movies is fun. It adds to the fun to try to discover scenes in which the laws of physics are ignored.

How fast is the universe expanding? The answer to that important question will also tell us how old it is, and what its final fate might be. Wendy Freedman leads a team at the Carnegie Institution of Washington that used redshift data from the Hubble Space Telescope to calculate the Hubble Constant. Their calculation was precise enough to let astronomers begin to answer those questions. In 1999, Freedman's team announced their finding that the universe is expanding at a rate that makes it about fourteen billion years old.

Born in Toronto, Canada, Wendy Freedman grew up in a family that encouraged her interest in science. Her father especially had a strong interest in astronomy, and introduced young Wendy to the sky.

Despite the family interest in astronomy, Wendy started her university career intending to major in biophysics. But an astronomy professor and a graduate assistant, both enthusiastic about astronomy, convinced Wendy to become an astronomer. She received her PhD from the University of Toronto in 1984, and shortly thereafter became the first woman to join the Carnegie Institution's permanent scientific staff.

# WENDY FREEDMAN

**born 1957**

When Freedman's team received time on the Hubble Telescope, they began their search for a precise Hubble Constant by looking in a galaxy named M100. There they hoped to find Cepheid variable stars to use as their study objects. After looking at four thousand stars over the course of sixty nights, they succeeded in identifying twenty Cepheids that would meet their needs.

Freedman's success in calculating a Hubble Constant would not

## Physical Constants

Astronomers often work with physical constants. The speed of light is one constant astronomers use. You may have come across constants in a math class. For example, the constant you use when you want to figure out the area or circumference of a circle is called Pi. The constant Pi has a value of about 3.14 and it relates the radius of a circle to its area and to its circumference. These two equations express these relationships:

A = Pi R² (which means the area equals Pi times the radius squared)

C = Pi D (which means the circumference equals Pi times the diameter)

No mater what size a circle is, Pi remains the same. This is why it is called a constant.

Suppose you and your friends want pizza, but you can't decide whether to order one large pizza or two mediums. The medium one is 10 inches across, and the large one is 20 inches across. To find the area of the pizzas, you need to know the radius of each. Since the radius is one-half the diameter, the medium pizza has a radius of 5, and the large pizza has a radius of 10.

Would you get more pizza if you ordered two 10-inch pizzas or one 20-inch pizza. Use the constant Pi to find the answer.

Take the formula for the area of a circle and plug in the radius of each pizza. For the smaller pizza, A = Pi(5)2, which equals 78.5 square inches. For the larger pizza, A = Pi (20)2, which equals 315 square inches. Now you can see that the large pizza gives you four times more than one medium. So, go ahead and order the large pizza. Left-over pizza makes a great snack, anyway.

Physical constants are important in all science. Astronomers are especially interested in the Hubble Constant, which relates the speed with which a galaxy is speeding away from us to how far away it already is.

have been possible without the power of the Hubble Telescope. Now she leads her team in designing and building another giant telescope, this one to stay on the ground. Named the Giant Magellan Telescope, it will contain seven 27.8-foot mirrors, and produce a resolving power at least ten times that of the Hubble.

One hope for the Giant Magellan is that it will be the first telescope powerful enough to be able to see an Earth-like planet beyond our solar system. Some astronomers estimate that at least twenty-five percent of all stars have planets. So the discovery of another Earthlike body may come soon after launch.

In reflecting on her career, Wendy Freedman said, "There isn't a day that goes by that I am not pleased with my decision to become a scientist. Some days I can't believe that I get paid to do what I love."

Her advice to students thinking about careers is to "find something that you like to do. Science is one option, and it is a very rewarding one. You have only one life, so it is worth taking the time to work hard, and to find something that you really enjoy doing." ◉

## Hubble Constant Applied

For the last fifty years of the twentieth century, astronomers worked hard to identify the exact size of the Hubble Constant, because it would tell them not only how far away a particular galaxy was but also the age of the universe.

Hubble's theory says that the velocity with which a galaxy is speeding away is equal to a constant times the distance of the galaxy away from the Earth.

$V = H_0 D$ (where H is the Hubble Constant, V is the velocity of the receding galaxy, and D is its distance from the Earth).

In 1999, Wendy Freedman used data from the Hubble Space Telescope to recalculate the Hubble Constant. The new value, 74 kilometers per second per megaparsec, suggests a universe that is old enough — about twelve billion years old — to contain the oldest stars. (A megaparsec is 3.26 light-years.) The value also suggests that the universe may expand forever, and seems to support the Big Bang theory of formation.

For many astronomers, the most important question facing the human race is, Are we alone? Since 1986, Jill Tarter has devoted her professional life to trying to answer that question.

*The existence of extraterrestrial intelligence ... is a truly fundamental question.*

*Jill Tarter*

# JILL CORNELL TARTER

**born 1944**

Fifteen-year-old Jill Cornell closed her book and thought about aliens. What would they be like? Would beings from other planets be bipedal like humans, would they walk on four legs, or would they fly, or move on wheels? How would they see? How would they communicate? The one question Jill Cornell never asked herself was, Do they exist? She always believed they did, and now she leads the team searching for them.

Growing up in New York state, Jill always thought she'd be a scientist. She just didn't know what kind of a scientist. "I don't have a very good long-term memory, so biology seemed out of the question," she said in an interview. And, although the family did a great deal of star-watching, especially from the beaches of southern Florida, she didn't consider a career in astronomy until later in her college career.

Growing up in a family that supported her interest in math and science left Tarter unprepared for her reception at Cornell. She applied to the college for the scholarship available to Cornell's descendants, which she is, only to find out that the scholarship was only for male descendants. Two days after being rejected for the Cornell scholarship, she received notice she had won a Procter & Gamble Co. Scholarship, the first woman to receive that engineering scholarship. Being the only woman in the engineering school was a challenge, but Tarter described it as a character-forming experience.

The summer of her junior year, Jill married and changed her name to Tarter. A year later, she headed to Berkeley for a doctorate in astrophysics, then to NASA at the Ames Research Center, where she did research on brown dwarf stars. Here she met scientists who were beginning to design a search for signals from extraterrestrial civilizations. "I fell in love with SETI [the Search for Extraterrestrial Intelligence]," she said.

In 1986, Tarter helped form the SETI Institute, to coordinate research. The institute was controversial from the beginning. In 1993, Congress stopped funding the project, using as one argument the fact that no one had discovered any other planets, so the search was a waste of money.

SETI is now funded with private money. The project uses radio telescopes to scan for signals originating from other intelligent beings. Plans are underway for larger radio telescopes, but the idea that most appeals to Tarter is building a radio telescope on the Moon. "Lunarecibo," as she calls it, would be built on the side of the Moon away from Earth. That site would protect the telescope from the barrage of radio signals from the Earth and allow better scanning. Once built, the Lunarecibo could be a robotic operation needing no attendants.

"There hasn't been a woman on the Moon yet," Tarter said. When Lunarecibo is built, she wants to be the woman who changes that.

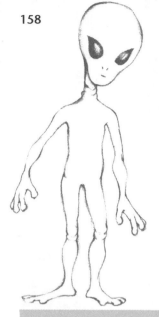

For her outstanding research and her effective representation of the SETI project, Jill Tarter was named one of the world's one hundred most "influential and powerful people" in 2004, by the editors of *Time* magazine.

"For me the important thing about detecting another intelligent species somewhere else in the universe is that it holds up a mirror to the Earth," she said. "And it says, 'OK humans, you're all humans.' And the differences between us and that [other] life form are vast, and they should trivialize the differences among humans that we find so hard to live with these days." ◉

## The Radio Telescope at Arecibo

Built in a natural hemispherical depression in the mountains of Puerto Rico, the world's largest single-dish radio telescope began operating in 1963. The 1000-foot-wide telescope is used to study pulsars, to map gases in the galaxy, and to bounce radiation off other planets in the solar system and record the reflections. The telescope has appeared in such movies as *Golden Eye,* a James Bond movie, and *Contact,* based on a book by Carl Sagan that describes the search for extraterrestrial intelligence.

Operated jointly by the National Astronomy and Ionosphere Center, the National Science Foundation, and NASA, the telescope is available for use to anyone in the world who submits an approved proposal.

# Rising Stars

The opening years of the twenty-first century finds many more women becoming astronomers. More powerful telescopes and new technology allows astronomers to observe from more parts of the globe. Astronomers now use telescopes at the North Pole and in orbit around Earth. And they plan telescopes for the far side of the Moon. Here are some of the new generation of astronomers and the questions they are asking about our universe.

**Victoria Kaspi**, at McGill University, in Montreal, Canada, uses radio waves and X-rays to study pulsars, a type of neutron star.

**Emily Levesque** discovered three of the largest stars known. Each star is over a billion miles in diameter and weighs in at more than twenty-five times our Sun. Now at the University of Hawaii, Emily continues to study the evolution of these enormous stars.

**Kris Blindert,** at the Max-Planck Institute in Heidelberg, Germany, studies the distribution of matter in galactic clusters. Not an easy job, she says, since the clusters are composed mostly of dark matter.

**Maggie Turnbull** looks for planets she thinks might contain signs of life, and has compiled a list of candidate planets. Currently at the Carnegie Institution Department of Terrestrial Magnetism, she works often at the radio telescope at Arecibo.

**Tesla Jeltema**, at the Carnegie Observatories, uses X-ray satellites and optical telescopes in Hawaii and Chile to study the formation of large structures in the universe containing as many as a thousand galaxies.

**Chung-Pei Ma**, at MIT, studies dark matter and superclusters. She tries to understand the distribution of matter in the universe.

**Andrea Ghez**, at UCLA, has confirmed the existence of a massive black hole at the center of our Milky Way Galaxy.

**Ekaterina A. Evstigneeva** *has degrees from St. Petersburg State University in Russia. Now she is at the University of Queensland, in Australia, where she studies ultra-compact dwarf galaxies and globular clusters.*

**Meg Urry** *chairs the Yale Physics Department and directs the Yale Center for Astronomy and Astrophysics. She studies the growth of supermassive black holes.*

**Marla Geha**, *at the Carnegie Observatories, studies the structure and dynamics of dwarf galaxies.*

**Susan Tereby** *discovered the first planet outside our solar system. By 2006, astronomers had found more than one hundred planets. Some astronomers estimate that one-fourth of all stars have planets.*

**Jogee Shardha**, at the University of Texas at Austin, researches the structure and behavior of disk galaxies from the time the universe was less than half its current age.

**You?**

**Kim Venn** is an Associate Professor in Physics and Astronomy at University of Victoria, and a Canada Research Chair. Her research aims to use the chemistry of old stars as a stellar fossil record to understand galaxy formation and evolution.

**Tania Ruiz** built her own decametric (tens of meters) radio telescope when she was a senior in high school, to detect emissions from the planet Jupiter. Now at the Center for Archaeoastronomy in College Park, Maryland, Ruiz, who is part Aztec, says her main interest is in the archaeology of Western Europe. This interest was spurred from her archaeological field work with the University of Leeds in England.

**Alicia Soderberg**, a doctoral student at Cal Tech, studies gamma-ray bursts from supernovae.

# Glossary

**Asteroids** Any of the small, irregular bodies orbiting the Sun.

**Astrolabe** An ancient instrument used to measure the altitude of a star, the Sun, or a planet. Astrolabes have been replaced by sextants.

**Astronomical canon** A list of stars, their locations, and their expected movements.

**Atheneum** A reading room or library. Also an institution that promotes learning.

**Atomic energy states** Star-like temperatures that cause changes in the energy of an atom. These changes appear as dark lines on spectrograms.

**Big Bang theory** The theory that the universe began when a single very hot point exploded, and has been expanding ever since.

**Binary star** A double-star system in which two stars orbit around a common center.

**Black hole** An object, usually a star, that has collapsed under its own weight to such small size and enormous density that its gravitational force does not allow even light to escape.

**Binary star** A double-star system in which two stars orbit around a common center.

**Catalog** A list of items. They are often arranged alphabetically and include descriptions. Star catalogs include a description of the star and its location at specific times.

**Celestial** Having to do with the sky or the heavens.

**Celestial mechanics** The study of the movement of stars, planets, galaxies, and other celestial bodies.

**Cepheid variables** A group of stars that vary from bright to dim and back to bright again. Each star changes over a specific time period. In general, the greater the brightness, the longer the time period.

**Charge-coupled device (CCD)** A device for forming electronic images. A layer of silicon releases electrons when it is struck by incoming light. The electronic image can be read and stored by a computer.

# Glossary

**Chronometer** An instrument to precisely measure the passage of time, a clock or watch. From *chrono* meaning time, and *meter*, to measure.

**Comet** Often called a dirty snowball. Many astronomers think comets are large chunks of frozen ammonia and hydrogen. As a comet approaches the Sun, the frozen material melts and streams away, making the tail we see.

**Comet sweeping** Scanning portions of the sky rapidly, looking for fuzzy objects that have appeared since the last scan.

**Cosmology** The study of the nature and evolution of the universe or cosmos.

**Cycles** A pattern of regularly occurring events. Summer occurs once each year. The tide is high twice a day.

**Dark matter** The theoretical mass that appears to be missing from the universe. Calculations of galactic velocities suggest that much more mass must be present than can be accounted for by the stars detected by telescopes. The fact that it is not visible leads astronomers to call it dark matter.

**Deploy** To place or position something.

**Doppler effect** In sound, the increase in pitch as a sound source comes toward the listener, and the decrease in pitch as the sound source recedes. In light, the Doppler effect also results in a change in wavelength. Light approaching the observer is shifted to shorter wavelengths — the redshift. Light receding from the observer is shifted to longer wavelengths and appears to shift to the blue end of the spectrum.

**Double stars** Stars that orbit a common center of mass, now called binary stars.

**Easter** The first Sunday after the first full Moon after the Spring Equinox.

**Eclipse** The elimination of light from one heavenly body by another. A solar eclipse occurs when the Earth passes through the shadow of the Moon, blocking our view of the Sun.

**Equinox** The time during the year when the length of the day and night are roughly equal. It is the time the Sun appears to move from one side of the equator to the other. Usually

# Glossary

this happens around March 21 for the Spring Equinox, and September 21 for the Autumnal Equinox.

**Extraterrestrial** Anything originating off the Earth, or Terra.

**G-force** Amount of gravitational force. One g equals the normal gravitational force. Shuttle crews normally experience as much as eight gravities on lift off.

**Galaxy** A large cluster of stars — between a million and hundreds of millions of stars, gas, and dust — held together by gravity.

**Gamma rays** Electromagnetic radiation of very short wave-length and high energy. Gamma rays are similar to X-rays, but of even higher energy.

**Geosynchronous orbit** A path around the Earth in which an object orbits at the same speed as the Earth revolves. In a geosynchronous orbit, an object stays above the same spot on the Earth's surface. Communications satellites are placed in geosynchronous orbit, at an altitude of 22,300 miles above the Earth.

**Glacial drift** Piles of rock and debris left when glaciers recede, following an ice age.

**Globular cluster** A large, spherical cluster of stars located in the halo of the galaxy.

**Hubble Space Telescope** The first orbiting optical telescope. The Hubble scans the heavens in infrared, visible, and ultraviolet wavelengths.

**Hubble Constant** A number that relates the apparent speed with which a galaxy recedes to its distance from the Milky Way. The constant includes factors for the density of the universe as well as the age of the universe.

**Infinite** Something that extends without an end.

**Infinitesimal** Infinitely small.

**Light year** The distance, usually in miles, that light travels in one year.

**Luminous** Bright or glowing.

**Luminosity** The brightness or intensity of a star.

# Glossary

**Meteorite** The remnant of a meteoroid that survives the fall through the Earth's atmosphere to reach the ground.

**Micro gravity** (micro-g) A fraction of an Earth gravity. When astronauts are in orbit around the Earth in a shuttle, or on a space station, they are nearly weightless, but not entirely. The gravity is small, but not zero. We call it micro gravity, or micro-g.

**NASA** The **N**ational **A**eronautic and **S**pace **A**dministration, the agency that develops and oversees American space programs.

**Natural philosophy** An early Greek term for the natural sciences. It included ethics and morality along with life sciences and physical sciences.

**Nebula** In Caroline Herschel's time, a nebula was any fuzzy spot in the sky. Many of those fuzzy objects turned out to be other galaxies, or star clusters, or gas clouds. Now nebula means a cloud of dust or gas.

**Nepotism** The practice of hiring one's relatives. Legislators enacted anti-nepotism rules, to prevent the practice. Since they mostly discriminated against women, they have been declared illegal in many states.

**Orbital mechanics** The study and calculation of the orbits of objects under the influence of the gravity of celestial bodies.

**Payload** Everything on the shuttle that is not needed for research, operations, or life support. The frogs, rats, and insects sent into space for study are payloads. So are satellites taken into orbit to be deployed in a specific orbit.

**Period** The time interval for some regular event to take place.

**Phase of the Moon** The monthly cycle of changes in the Moon's appearance, as seen from the Earth.

**Photometry** The study of the brightness of stars.

**Pulsar** A rapidly rotating neutron star that emits periodic pulses of electromagnetic radiation.

**Quasar** An acronym for a quasi-stellar, or star-like, object. These objects exhibit very

# Glossary

large redshifts. They must be moving very rapidly and lie at the farthest reaches of detection. Quasars may have formed in the earliest stages of the universe.

**Radar** An acronym for **ra**dio **d**irection **a**nd **r**ange. Radar devices transmit high-frequency radio waves and detect the reflected beam showing the distance and direction of an object.

**Radio astronomy** A study of the radio waves emitted naturally by objects in space. One of the first sources of radio waves detected was the center of our own galaxy.

**Sextant** An instrument used to measure the angular distance between two objects, such as the horizon and a heavenly body. Sextants are used to determine latitude at sea.

**Solstice** The moment when the Sun reaches its farthest northern point (summer solstice) or southern point (winter solstice).

**Spectrum** The array of colors or wavelengths that make up electromagnetic radiation. Spectra (plural of spectrum) are produced when radiation is dispersed by passing it through a prism, or bouncing it off a diffraction grating.

**Stellar** About stars.

**Suffrage** The right or privilege of voting, also called the franchise.

**Survey** To measure and calculate land areas, and to locate and establish boundaries for mapping purposes.

**Telemetry** Automatic radio transmissions from space probes, satellites, and other space-going vehicles.

**Trigonometry** The branch of mathematics that deals with the relationship between the lengths of sides and the angles of triangles.

**Variable Stars** Stars that vary in brightness.

**Wavelength** The distance between two crests on successive waves. The wavelength of light determines its color.

# References

## Chapter One

Alic, Margaret, *Hypatia's Heritage,* Boston: Beacon Press, 1986.

Cooney, Miriam P., Ed., *Celebrating Women in Mathematics and Science,* Reston: The National Council of Teachers, 1999.

Dzielska, Marie, *Hypatia of Alexandria,* Cambridge: Harvard University Press, 1995.

Flanagan, Sabrina, *Hildegard of Bingen, 1098–1179: A Visionary Life,* London: Routledge Press, 1991.

Meador, Betty De Shong, *Inanna, Lady of Largest Heart, Poems of the Sumerian High Priestess Enheduanna,* Austin: University of Texas Press, 2000.

Ogilvie, Marilyn Bailey, *Women in Science: Antiquity Through the Nineteenth Century: A Biographical Dictionary,* Cambridge: MIT Press, 1986.

Vu, Jennie Ngoc, *Queen Sondok,* Pacific University's Portal On Korea web site.

## Chapter Two

Alic, Margaret, *Hypatia's Heritage,* Boston: Beacon Press, 1986.

Herschel, Caroline, *Memoir and Correspondence,* Mary Herschel, ed., Appleton: Appleton Press, 1876.

Hoskin, Michael, *The Herschel Partnership: As Viewed by Caroline,* Cambridge, England: Science History Publications, 2003.

Stille, Darlene, *Extraordinary Women Scientists,* New York: Children's Press, 1995.

Veglahn, Nancy, *Women Scientists,* New York: Facts on File, 1991.

## Chapter Three

Burke, James, *The Day the Universe Changed,* New York: Little Brown,1985.

Gormley, Beatrice, *Maria Mitchell: The Soul of an Astronomer,* Grand Rapids: Eerdman's, 1995.

James, Edward T.,Ed., *Notable American Women: A Biographical Dictionary,* Cambridge: Harvard University Press, 1971.

Kass-Simon, G., and Farnes, Patricia, Eds., *Women of Science: Righting the Record,* Bloomington: Indiana U. Press, 1990.

Morgan, Helen L., *Maria Mitchell, First Lady of American Astronomy,* Philadelphia: Westminster Press, 1977.

# References

Sobel, Dava, *Longitude: The True Story of a Lone Genius Who Solved the Greatest Scientific Problem of His Time*, London: Walker and Co., 1995.

Wright, Helen, *Sweeper in the Sky: The Life of Maria Mitchell,* New York: Macmillan,1949.

## Chapter Four

Edward, James, T., Ed., *Notable American Women: A Biographical Dictionary,* Cambridge: Harvard University Press, 1971.

Greenstein, George, *Portraits of Discovery,* New York: John Wiley, 1998.

Johnson, George, *Miss Leavitt's Stars: The Untold Story of the Woman Who Discovered How to Measure the Universe*, New York: Atlas Books, 2005.

Kass-Simon, G., and Farnes, Patricia, Eds., *Women of Science: Righting the Record,* Bloomington: Indiana University Press, 1990.

## Chapter Five

Haramundanis, Katherine, Ed., *Cecilia Payne-Gaposchkin: An Autobiography and Other Recollections,* Cambridge, England: Cambridge University Press, 1984, 1996.

Greenstein, George, *Portraits of Discovery,* New York: John Wiley, 1998.

Hogg, Helen Sawyer, *The Stars Belong to Everyone: How to Enjoy Astronomy,* Toronto: Doubleday Canada, 1976.

Kass-Simon, G., and Farnes, Patricia, Eds., *Women of Science: Righting the Record,* Bloomington: Indiana U. Press, 1990.

## Chapter Six

Bartusiak, M.,"The Woman Who Spins the Stars*,"* *Discover*, Oct. 1990.

Blackburn, Harriet B., "Milky Way Absorbs Scholar," *Christian Science Monitor*, June 13, 1957.

Hunter, Deidre & Rubin, Vera, "Women Worldwide in Astronomy," Jan/Feb 1992 Volume 21, #1

Knapp, Gillian, "Charting the Infrared Sky," *Sky & Telescope Magazine,* August, 1997.

Rubin, Vera, *Bright Galaxies, Dark Matters,* Melville, Long Island: AIP Press, 1996.

Interview with Nancy Roman, *Christian Science Monitor,* June 13, 1957, *New York Times,* Feb. 6, 1962.

# References

## Chapter Seven

Bailey, Martha, *American Women in Science: 1950 to the Present*, Santa Barbara: ABC-CLIO, 1998.

Bartusiak, Marcia, "Mapping the Universe," *Discover*, August 1990.

Bertsch McGrayne, Sharon, *Nobel Prize Women in Science: Their Lives, Struggles and Momentous Discoveries*, Secaucus: Carol Publishing, 1998.

Kolb, Rocky, *Blind Watchers of the Sky*, Addison Wesley, U.S. and Canada, 1996.

"Margaret Geller," *Current Biography*, New York: H.W. Wilson Co., 1997.

Geller, Margaret, personal correspondence, 1999.

Greenstein, George, *Portraits of Discovery*, New York: John Wiley, 1998.

Hill, Edward, *My Daughter Beatrice: A Personal Memoir of Dr. Beatrice Tinsley, Astronomer*, Washington, D.C.: The American Physical Society, 1986.

Powell, Corey S. "Up Against the Wall," *Scientific American*, February 1990.

"S. Jocelyn Bell Burnell," *Current Biography*, New York: H.W. Wilson Co., 1995.

Wade, Nicholas, "A Graduate Student's Story," *Science, August 1975, Volume 189*

Yount, Lisa, *Women in Math and Science: A Biographical Dictionary*, New York: Facts on File, 1999.

## Chapter Eight

Briggs, Carole S., *Women in Space*, Minneapolis: Lerner Publications, 1988.

Caldwell, Jean, "Ride Urges Women to Study Math," *Boston Globe*, June 30, 1985.

Heppenheimer, T.A., *Countdown: A History of Space Flight*, New York: John Wiley & Sons, 1997.

Hurwitz, Jane, & Hurwitz, Sue, *Sally Ride: Shooting for the Stars*, New York: Fawcett Ballantine, 1989.

*Parade Magazine*, December 11, 2005 (Sally Ride quote)

Renehan Jr., Edward J., *Science on the Web*, Springer-Verlag, 1996.

"Sally Ride, Ph.D.," *Health,* 1985.

"Sally Ride," *Current Biography*, New York: H.W. Wilson Co., 1983.

# Picture Credits

**Cover**

Sam Pitts (starry sky); Niki Harris (girl at telescope)

*vi, viii:* NASA and The Hubble Heritage Team (STScI/AURA)

## Chapter One

*1:* NASA, ESA, and A. Nota (STScI/ESA)

*5:* Niki Harris

*3, 9, 11:* Toni Bertoloni

## Chapter Two

*13:* Niki Harris

*18:* Courtesy Smithsonian Institution

*20:* NASA and The Hubble Heritage Team (STScI/AURA)

*21:* NASA, ESA and The Hubble Heritage Team (STScI/AURA)

*22:* Courtesy William Herschel Museum, Bath, England

*25:* NOAO/Tod R. LauerNOAO/Kris Koenig

*27:* Royal Astronomical Society/Photo Researchers, Inc.

*26:* Poem by permission of author Siv Cedering

*28:* Hubblesite.org/newscenter, M. Jäger & G. Rhemann

## Chapter Three

*29:* Maria Mitchell at the telescope in 1851 in an oil painting by Hermoine Dassel. Courtesy Maria Mitchell Museum, Nantucket

*32:* Courtesy Maria Mitchell Museum, Nantucket

*35:* 1910 photograph, Lowell Observatory/NOAO/AURA/NSF

*38, 39, 40:* Courtesy Vassar College Libraries

## Chapter Four

*41:* Courtesy of Harvard University Archives

*42:* Courtesy of Harvard University Archives [HUP Fleming, Williamina (5a)]

*43:* Keystone View Company stereoscopic image, collection of John Bauguess

*45, 47, 62:* Niki Harris

*50:* Wellesley College Library Archives

*52:* Courtesy AIP Emilio Segre Visual Archives, Shapley Collection; Courtesy of Harvard University Archives [HUGFP 125.82p Box 2]

*53:* Courtesy of Harvard University Archives [HUP Leavitt, Henrietta Swan (1a)]

*54:* Harvard College Observatory, courtesy AIP Emilio Segre Visual Archives

*56:* AIP Emilio Segre Visual Archives

*60:* Courtesy of Harvard University Archives [HUP Maury, Antonia Caetano (1b)]

*63:* Courtesy of Harvard University Archives [HUV 985 (4-2)]

## Chapter Five

*65:* Courtesy AIP Emilio Segre Visual Archives, Shapley Collection

*67:* Courtesy of the artist, Patricia Watwood

*68:* Toni Bertolini

*71:* Courtesy of Harvard University Archives [HUP Payne-Gaposhkin, Cecilia (2)]

*75:* Courtesy AIP Emilio Segre Visual Archives, Shapley Collection

*77:* Mt. Holyoke College Library Archives

*79:* University of Toronto Archives, courtesy AIP Emilio Segre Visual Archives

*80:* Canada Science and Technology Museum

*82:* Robert T. Rood, Astronomy Department, University of Virginia; The Hubble Heritage Team (AURA/STScI/NASA)

## Chapter Six

*83:* Door 205, from the "collection of undistinguished photographs on doors of IGPP

*84:* Courtesy Franklin Delano Roosevelt Library

*86:* Courtesy UC London

*87:* UCLA Dept of Physics and Astronomy

*88:* Chris Parker

*90:* AIP Emilio Segre Visual Archives

*91:* Courtesy G. Knapp; Courtesy Fermilab Visual Media Services

*93:* Courtesy Dr. Nancy G. Roman; NASA

*95:* Courtesy Smithsonian Astrophysical Observatory

# Picture Credits

*96:* NASA/MSFC (Skylab); NASA/GSFC (rocket); NASA

*97:* NASA; Photo by Lyndi Schrecengost, courtesy of Retired Scientists, Engineers & Technicians, ©2006

*98:* NASA/SM2 : STS-82

*99:* Courtesy Vassar College Libraries

*101:* Tamar Thibodeau (photo)

*102:* Courtesy Robert Rubin

*103:* Carnegie Institution of Washington

*104:* Kent Ford

*105:* Arvydas Cetyrkovskis

*107:* Mark Godfrey

*108:* Private collection of Vera Rubin

*109:* Courtesy Robert Rubin

*110:* Courtesy A. Pasten, A. Gomez, NOAO/AURA/NSF

## Chapter Seven

*111:* Courtesy Yale University

*112:* Courtesy the Franklin Delano Roosevelt Library

*113, 115:* Toni Bertolini

*114:* NASA, ESA, M. Robberto (Space Telescope Science Institute/ESA) and the Hubble Space Telescope Orion Treasury Project Team

*116:* NASA/ESA (spiral); NASA, ESA and The Hubble Heritage Team (STScI/AURA) (dwarf)

*117:* NASA/STScI (cluster); Magellan/U.Arizona/D.Clowe et al.; NASA, ESA and The Hubble Heritage Team (STScI/AURA) (ring)

*118:* NASA and The Hubble Heritage Team (STScI/AURA) (colliding)

*120:* NOAO

*121:* The Open University, courtesy AIP Emilio Segre Visual Archives

*122:* Armagh Observatory

*123:* Jocelyn Bell Burnell

*125:* Bill Saxton NRAO/AUI/NSF

*128:* University of London Observatory; Todd Boroson/NOAO/AURA/ NSF, NASA, ESA, S. Beckwith (STScI), and The Hubble Heritage Team STScI/AURA)

*129, 133:* Margaret Geller

*134:* Niki Harris

*135:* NASA Astrophysics Data System

## Chapter Eight

*137:* USGS – Gene Shoemaker

*138:* Hubble Space Telescope Comet Team, John Clarke, University of Michigan and NASA

*141:* USGS – G and C Shoemaker, D Levy

*142:* Asteroid Ida: NASA/JPL

*143:* Marie Aguilar; Johnson Space Center Digital Image Collection

*144:* NASA Photo ID: AS15-86-11603

*146:* NASA/JSC

*147:* NASA

*149:* NASA/KSC

*151:* Nick Ewing

*153:* Carnegie Observatories

*156:* SETI Institute

*157:* Anthony Holloway

*158:* Toni Bertolini (alien); Courtesy NAIC/Arecibo Observatory, a facility of the NSF

## Chapter Nine

*163:* (Jogee Shardha) Matt Lankes

Other photos courtesy of subjects

*Page numbers in italic type refer to illustrations.*
*Page numbers followed by letter n refer to timeline notes.*

# ABOUT THE AUTHOR

While spending her first eight years on remote construction sites where her father built highways and dams, Mabel Armstrong's playmates were often lizards, garter snakes, and the family of pack rats given her by a local logger. Her attachment to nature and biology continued until she fell in love with chemistry in high school. About the same time, she discovered science fiction and was the only girl in her high school who read the tiny collection in the school library. Ignoring teachers and counselors who discouraged her interest in science, Mabel majored in chemistry in college where she was often the only girl in a 200-student lecture room. When interviewed by a major petroleum company after graduation, she was told, "Women are not allowed in the laboratories, they work in the library doing patent searches." An international food products company said, "You have just the training we're looking for, but we know women marry and leave. So we don't hire women."

Mabel taught college chemistry for twenty-five years. She now lives in rural Oregon where she still reads science fiction and is hard at work on the next Discovering Women in Science book, about women chemists.